Malcolm Gluck is the author of *Superplonk*, the best-selling annual guide to supermarket wines. He writes the enormously popular Superplonk column in *Weekend Guardian*, a monthly wine column for the Scottish *Sunday Post Magazine*, and is wine editor of *Cosmopolitan*. He is also consultant wine editor of *Sainsbury's Magazine* and has written for *She*, *Country Living*, *Independent on Sunday*, *Today* and the *Sunday Express*. He often appears on TV and speaks on radio. He is also the author (along with Antony Worrall Thompson) of *Supernosh*.

GW00692388

GLUCK'S GUIDE

High Street Wines 1995

MALCOLM GLUCK

faber and faber
LONDON · BOSTON

First published in 1994
by Faber and Faber Limited
3 Queen Square London WC1N 3AU

Photoset by Parker Typesetting Service, Leicester
Printed in England by Clays Ltd, St Ives plc

© Malcolm Gluck, 1994

Malcolm Gluck is hereby identified as author of this work in accordance
with Section 77 of the Copyright, Designs and Patents Act 1988

A CIP record for this book is available from the British Library

ISBN 0-571-17373-X

10 9 8 7 6 5 4 3 2

TO DAVID OFFENBACH,
for his friendship

Contents

Introduction

You could say that this book has been a lifetime in the writing. Its genesis can be traced back to experiences earlier than those which inspired the companion volume to this one, *Superplonk*. That book concerns itself exclusively with the wines on sale in supermarkets, and the first supermarket wine I tasted was a red Côtes du Rhône which Marks and Spencer were planning to put on sale. It was their first venture into wine retailing and the year, I think, was 1973. My unadulterated delight at finding this wine superb, and the price risibly low, was not the slightest bit mitigated by the thought that in order to buy it I would have to brave the bra and knicker shelves which was the merchandise we men, at that time, believed this store dealt in exclusively. I was pleased at the thought of the undergarment jungle I would have to negotiate in order to reach the bottle, not because I have any special interest in this area (above that of any normal heterosexual man's), but because I reckoned its situation would deter most male drinkers and thus I would be assured of a fully stocked shelf whenever I felt the need for a cheap and brilliant red Rhône. I tell you this so that you may be in no doubt of the lengths I will go to in order to find a bargain.

It was, however, wine merchants of the kind which fill this book who satisfied my first lust for wine – a lust which was first aroused by my witnessing a Frenchwoman at table in Gaillac thirty years ago. This arousal brought me, once back in England, quickly to the door of Oddbins, a newly outfitted enterprise (barely half a shop really) in Monmouth Street in the Seven Dials district of London – a seamy area – made infamous by Agatha Christie, which is cheek by jowl with

Covent Garden. Oddbins in those days was what it said it was – odd bins. The huge mercantile love affairs conducted by brewers with many independent wine dealers who had struggled to make ends meet after the war resulted in take-overs, and the neat and tidy brewers didn't care for all the thousands of odd bins they found in these merchants' messy cellars. So the 1960s were marked by regular auctions at which these wines, almost invariably from unfashionable châteaux or unheard-of vineyards, many of venerable vintages, a lot in half-bottle, a number in magnum- and jeroboam-sized bottles, were sold off. The man who started Oddbins snapped them up and built a business. I remember a half-bottle of 1928 Château Smith-Haut-Lafite I bought for fifteen bob under the impression that it must at least be a cousin of the great Lafite itself, which of course it wasn't. This wine turned out to be vinegar and did indeed make a component of a vinaigrette after the shop refused to take the bottle back or recompense me. Quite rightly it was pointed out that the risks attendant upon my wager were made clear to me as a condition of purchase when I gambled by buying the wine in the first place.

There is less of a gamble about buying wine from wine shops nowadays, not only because none of the shops represented in this book would be daft enough to flog thirty-six-year-old claret in halves, but also they have a faster turnover of the wines they do sell, the wines themselves are better made, and the buying skills of the professional buyers working for these retailers are higher than they have ever been.

However, what I continue to find so astonishing after completing all the research to write this book (i.e. boozing, boozing and yet more boozing) is that so many people still cannot get it into their noddles that decent, drinkable, even exciting and reasonably complex wines can be found for £3 and under. Years before I wrote about wine and became that peculiar species of humanity called a wine correspondent, I was buying and enjoying extremely cheap wines from wine shops and supermarkets. You would think, wouldn't you, that in this day and age, after five years of the worst recession since 1929 having wrought profound societal change, especially to middle-class life-styles, with off-licences collapsing, pubs changing, posh restaurants offering £12 multi-course lunches, and small wine merchants dying faster than mayflies, that the dunderheads among us, especially those who sell wine for a living and those who write about it, would have woken up to the simple fact that TERRIFIC WINES ARE AVAIL-ABLE IN THIS LAND FOR THREE QUID AND LESS and that WINE DRINKERS ENJOY PAYING LITTLE FOR A DECENT TIPPLE. Yet the March 1994 edition of *Which Wine Monthly* could announce, in slightly astonished tones as if some recently discovered truth was at last being revealed to the world, that 'you can buy some seriously good wine and still have change from £3', in spite of the UK's swingeing duty level. Indeed, such was their shock at discovering under-£3 wines that they actually miscalculated this duty level, claiming it was £1.02 instead of the official £1.01, but in their excite-ment this is a forgivable lapse. The Royal Appointees Corney and Barrow made no such error, however, in a pamphlet sent to its customers revealing that it too had woken up to cheap wine, and so it set about warning its customers off the filthy stuff. The ruse employed was to demonstrate that the duty on an expensive bottle (in which Corney and Barrow specializes) was the same as on a cheap bottle (in which C & B does not). This unarguable premise was followed by this clincher: 'On a scale, therefore, it makes more sense to spend, say, £10 on a bottle of wine where £1.01 is a substantially smaller propor-tion of total cost, than it would be on a bottle costing £2.50.'

At this point even the sober logician is trying not to fall off his chair laughing, but then the firm coolly goes on: 'We do not suggest that everyone should spend £10 on a bottle of wine, but we do emphatically suggest that £3.50 is the minimum that anyone should spend if they prefer to pay more for wine rather than duty and other costs.' The preference implied here, and which underpins the whole argument, is that it is better to spend more on wine because that way proportionately more goes to the wine merchant than to the Exchequer and other middle men. Never have I heard so fallacious an argument for why anyone should buy expensive wine. If only Corney and Barrow had taken the trouble to examine what value for money means where a greater outlay is involved, rather than trying to defend the indefensible, then they might have a case. There is absolutely nothing wrong with a £10 bottle of wine if it *carries proportionately a greater level of value than a £3 bottle* and if C & B has such wines – complex, rich, multi-dimensional – then it ought to trumpet these. The problem as I see it is that too many of the tenner bottles I taste (and I have not tasted C & B's wines, so I cannot comment on them specifically) aren't worth anywhere near that amount of money because they do not carry the greater value of increased complexity of fruit and thus offer deeper levels of pleasure in their consumption. This, and only this, is the argument that will wash where wine costing £10 is concerned.

I do not like the level of duty on wine and believe it should be drastically reduced, even if it means putting VAT on products VAT-free at present, but that said, I would rather give one-third of a £3 wine to the Exchequer than proportionately more of a £10 wine to an Old World wine producer who turns out over-priced, over-extracted, over-cropped rubbish with an impressive-sounding label. One reason why I like modern high-street wine retailers so much is that they concern themselves with fewer and fewer of these wines because they understand the value-for-money argument so well.

I was the first wine writer to concern himself so actively with the wonderful world of the bargain bottle and the encouragement I receive daily via my postbag disciplines my focus, maintains my resolve, and keeps my nose firmly in the glass. The fact is that the old-fashioned world of wine in the United Kingdom (buying, selling *and* critical appreciation) is still doddering under the mandate of a received wisdom which is as laughably out-of-date as a starting-handle on a motor car. The wine establishment and its lackeys still cannot bear the idea (indeed, in some cases close their eyes to the very fact) that the pillars which support so many of its long-held, cherished ideals are mildewed and seriously riddled with cracks. The idea that the only decent wine comes from old-established sites in famous European wine areas, is dead on its lees. It was dying long before I came along. I have merely nailed down the coffin.

The New World is replacing the Old, as did the emergent Barbarian the corrupt Roman. Anyone who screamed 'the Australians are at the gates!' twelve years ago would have been laughed at by the bordelais as they would have chuckled in patronizing glee at the suggestion that Corbières, just a few hundred miles away, would in the early 1990s be turning out superb wines of a multi-layered appeal and rich fruitiness to rival many of their own. The difference between the Old World and the New (and I mean by this not just new vineyards in far continents, but unfashionable areas in Europe both west and east) is vast. The Old is anxious to preserve a status quo based on ancient perceptions, not modern realities; the New is concerned with the world as it is now and this means doing things which suit the consumer's taste and pocket, not merely the maker's convenience. The Old World of wine is riddled with ridiculous rituals which do nothing but perpetuate mediocrity, while the New World initiates events which instrumentally improve quality year after year. The Burgundian *Confrérie des Chevaliers du Taste-vin*, for example, is a hollow public-relations extravaganza which actually retards progress, compared with the exciting and hugely informed wine shows which dominate the Australian wine scene and allow brilliant innovations to take place. As a guest judge at the 1994 McLaren Vale wine show in South Australia, I can testify personally to the influence these shows have, and how informed and influential are the participants. Compared with events like these, much of the Old World of wine's posturing is crippling progress. A New Zealand wine-maker, who puts together some of the best value and tastiest Chardonnay, Sauvignon Blanc, Merlot and Cabernet Sauvignon on sale in Britain, told me that when he visited an old-established French red-wine region, Beaujolais, for the first time, he was dumbfounded at the growers' ignorance of the outside world and shocked at some of their practices. Is it a coincidence that imports of French wine into this country have fallen for the fifth year in succession? That sales of New World wines have expanded? That wine growers in the Moselle are packing up in droves and those who do survive will only do so as long as Poland stays backward and its inhabitants are happy to find work as German grape-pickers at harvest time? That wine merchants who deal in such outmoded ideas as wine futures and concentrate purely on famous European vineyards have there gone to the wall or have been forced seriously to rethink their lists?

I am not necessarily pleased to report any of these things. I love France, its culture, and many of its wines – many of the reds of the Rhône and the whites of Alsace are among the most satisfyingly made and the most satisfyingly priced wines you can buy. I adore the wines of the Moselle as among the greatest expressions of human genius. And there are several specialist wine merchants without whom I should be poorer in knowledge and less rich in past pleasures. However, my first duty is to my readers' pockets and I put their money where my mouth is. When it comes to tasting wine, value for money makes as much impression upon me as fruit. Having a nose for a bargain helps as much as a nose for bouquet.

The unpretentious wine shop is a delight to the down-to-earth wine drinker because it ignores established ways and tread its own path, its credo being to satisfy its customers' needs where wine is a value-for-money purchase, not a symbol of status, power, or class. The result is that the British wine drinker is able to enjoy the widest range of wines from more countries than anyone else in the world. It is scandalous, of course, that the duty placed on wine by a venal Exchequer is as anomalous as that car starting-handle, but this is only to be expected when the musty old men who run this particular arm of government are the same ones who rejoice in the old values of wine as an expensive, reverential status symbol, not a simple, joyous and cheaply available expression of everyday ordinary life.

This is a hobby horse, that outrageous duty rate, and I don't apologize for mounting it twice in one introduction. My stable, however, contains other equally well-ridden steeds and one of them is the ritual of wine tastings themselves. Were you to attend such a gathering, in which so-called expert palates gather to gargle and spit, you would be amazed. How, you would ask yourself, can any sensible human being reach a decision about a wine's worth among such a rabble and amid such babble? Well, it is not easy and practice is essential – as it is to achieve the smoothest golf-swing and the perfect soufflé.

But the wine writer who can not only accurately assess a great many wines (and some tastings parade several hundred bottles) under such conditions, but also give consideration to the value for money of each and its suitability to certain foods, is an extremely rare animal indeed. For these reasons, I do not work under the same conditions as other wine writers.

I write in a basement without distraction, except that provided by the knocking on the door of delivery men bearing new wines for me to taste and the occasional intrusion of the clatter of minute fingers on the piano situated on the floor above. Behind me is a minute kitchen where I can prepare food to eat with the wines I wish to sample. Above me is the kitchen of the whole house where family and friends are entertained and fed, and where I put further to the test many of those wines I wish to examine more closely. Nothing changes a wine's personality like the food that is eaten with it and many of the wines within these pages have been subjected to such partnerships. I am extremely suspicious of the human palate in all situations except the most natural and mundane and if a wine gives me pleasure in a tasting among many-score others, I expect it to do so among friends and food. I prefer to make a final judgement on many wines in circumstances where there is as little artificiality as possible. The greatest insult you can hurl at me is to consider me a connoisseur. I am a simple enthusiast. And it is my enthusiasm I wish to communicate. My tastes, my opinions, are my own, and there's an end on't.

How this guide works
Each retailer in this Guide is separately listed alphabetically. Each has its own introduction with the wines logically arranged by country of origin, red and white (including rosés). Each wine's name is as printed on its label. The abbreviation

n.v. (non-vintage) indicates that no date is given on the label.

Each wine is rated on points out of 20. In practice, wines scoring fewer than 10 points are not included although sometimes, because a particular bottle has really got my goat and scored so miserably I feel readers might be amused by its inclusion, I stick in a low-pointer. An excellent wine can be so characterized because of its price, not only because it is rewarding to drink. Therefore, value for money is the basis of my whole approach to rating a wine. I expect expensive wines to be good, but I do not always expect good wines to be expensive. Thus, a brilliant £10 bottle may not offer better value than a £3 wine because, although the pricier wine is more impressive it is not, in my eyes, anywhere near three times as impressive.

The full scoring system, from my initial tasting and scoring point of view, works as follows:

20   Is outstanding and faultless in all departments: smell, taste and finish in the throat. Worth the price, even if you have to take out a second mortgage.

19   A superb wine. Almost perfect.

18   An excellent wine of clear complexity but lacking the sublime finesse for the top. Fabulously good value.

17   An exciting, well-made wine at an affordable price.

16   Very good wine indeed. Good enough for *any* dinner party. Not expensive.

15   For the money, a great mouthful with real style.

14   The top end of everyday drinking wine. Well-made and to be seriously recommended at the price.

13   Good wine, not badly made. Not great, but very drinkable.

12   Everyday drinking wine at a sensible price.

11   Drinkable, but not a wine to dwell on.

10   Average wine (at a low price), yet still a passable mouth-
      ful. Also, wines which are expensive and, though drink-
      able, do not justify their high price.

9   Cheap plonk. Acceptable for parties in dustbin-sized
      dispensers.

8   Rough stuff. Feeble value.

7   Good for pickling onions.

6   Hardly drinkable except by desperate thirsts on an icy
      night by a raging bonfire.

5   Wine with all its defects and mass manufacturing
      methods showing.

4   Not good at any price.

3   A palate polluter and barely drinkable.

2   Rat poison. Not to be recommended to anyone, even
      winos.

1   Beyond the pale. Awful. Even Lucretia Borgia wouldn't
      serve it.

For easy reference a condensed version of these ratings is to
be found on the very last page of the book.

Prices

I cannot guarantee the price of any wine in this Guide for all
the usual trite reasons: inflation, economic conditions over-
seas, the narrow margins on some supermarket wines making
it difficult to maintain consistent prices for very long and, of

course, the existence of those freebooters at the Exchequer who are liable to up taxes which the supermarkets cannot help but pass on to the consumer. To get around this problem, a price banding code is assigned to each wine:

A Under £2.50   B £2.50–3.50   C £3.50–5
D £5–7   E £7–10   F £10–13
G £13–20   H Over £20

I owe the following people my thanks for helping to make this book possible: Sarah Lutyens and Felicity Rubinstein, Sarah Gleadell and Belinda Matthews, and Linda Peskin.

Booths

'Five generations have spat into that,' said Edwin Booth proudly, indicating the copper spittoon beside the table on which sat 130 bottles of choice wine. Apparently, I was only the second wine writer to appear before the slightly warped, heavily pitted receptacle. Booths, of Preston, Lancs, do not, it seems, get many visitors from the wine-writing fraternity and this is a great pity.

However, this small northern supermarket chain rather grandly announces the company (which to give it its proper name is E. H. Booth & Co Ltd) to be 'High Class Supermarkets, Tea and Coffee Blenders, Wine and Spirit Merchants' and yet in spite of this it was the egalitarian readers of the *Guardian* who first pestered me to try its wines. They have twenty-two stores, mostly in Lancashire but with one in Cheshire and two in Cumbria, with another on the way in West Cumbria this year. These stores vary from biggies with 26,000 square feet to titchy ones with 3,000 square feet. The wine range offered in each store differs according to the size of the store and 'the demographic profile of the customer base'.

It is the only one of all the retailers I deal with where the person I talk to is an eponymous relative of the founder. Mr Edwin Booth has a wine list to be proud of and it is comprehensive enough to make any wine drinker's mouth open wide with surprise and drool with expectation.

The length of the list which inspires this difficult facial response is 16 feet 2 inches long – as the computer print-out runs – and covers scores of Bordeaux (red and white), Burgundy (ditto), Rhône (ditto), Loire, Alsace, Gascony and the Languedoc-Roussillon, Champagne, Germany, Italy, Spain

(Rioja, Navarra, Duero and Penedes), England, the USA
(California of course, but also New York State), Chile,
Argentina, Australia, New Zealand, Israel, Lebanon, South
Africa, Greece, Hungary, Bulgaria, Yugoslavia and Portugal.
Close on a thousand wines in various shapes, forms and bottle
sizes (getting on for twice as many as competitors ten times its
size). As I first regarded this list as it tumbled out of my hands
and fell to the floor, I felt a mixed sense of awe and despair.
How could I drink my way through this little lot? I'd have to
decamp to Preston for a month.

And look at some of the wines I'd have to negotiate:
Château Margaux '78 (£82.85), Bâtard-Montrachet '88
(£79.99), Hermitage Grippat '89 (£22.99), Gewürtztraminer
Cuvée Anne '89 (£35.95), Brunello Montalcino '70 (£36.53),
Sassicaia '90 (£38.50), Opus 1 '81 (£42.39), Penfolds Grange
Hermitage '87 (£31.49), Louis Roederer Crystal Brut '83
(£49.95) and Taylor's Port '77 (£44.99). What were these
wines doing in Preston, Lancs? What were *Guardian* readers
thinking of in asking me to hob-nob with a shop which sold
such wines?

When I finally took the plunge and arranged to meet the
purveyors, I expected to be greeted at the very least by a
pomaded Dickensian codger with white whiskers, a Pickwick-
ian waistcoat complete with fob watch and notebook, and
walking with a significant list to the right caused by a lifetime
of carrying a portmanteau of old claret samples with which to
tempt the rich, four-poster-bedridden squires who surely
formed the firm's solid customer base.

Things didn't quite work out like that. True, I did spit in
the old copper pot under the eye of Mr Booth's great-great-
grandad, also an Edwin and who started the store in 1846 and
died in 1899, but Edwin-past would have been astonished at
the New World wines Edwin-present is pleased to enthuse

about. Doubtless the crook who broke into the premises the night before I arrived and stole away with an antique clock would have been despatched to Australia had he committed the same crime 150 years ago. As it is, Booths have one of the tastiest Australian shirazes I ever set lips upon (see entry under Normans) and so the store's customers are obviously not the stick-in-the-muds prejudice might suppose. That said, however, there is no doubting this company's respect for tradition (which in the north of England at least has always gone hand-in-hand with value for money).

'We are preoccupied with the raw materials for cooking as well as wine,' I was told and discovered that this preoccupation stretches to wanting to know which wines go best with which foods. As a result, they tested out, for instance, certain wines with a selection of their own marinated meats for sale to barbecue cooks. Did you know chiantis don't take well to barbecued food? Not in Lancashire, they don't. But riojas are in their element, as are Argentinian cabernet sauvignons. Booths, as well as offering this sort of advice, also offer 185 cheeses.

However, in one respect Edwin-present has no truck with modern notions. Certain of the ideas debated in the introduction to this year's *Superplonk* book concerning screwcaps replacing corks in wine bottles were dismissed with contempt. 'Part of the thrill of wine, sinking a corkscrew into a cork,' I was advised. 'Absolutely no alternative to cork.'

Hmm. We'll see.

AUSTRALIAN WINE – *red*

Brown Brothers Tarrango 1993   15   £C
Vivid, striking, softly smoky and rubbery, and so gluggable it's
sinful.

**Dalwhinnie Moonamber Cabernet Sauvignon
1988**   14   £E

Denham Estate Shiraz n.v.   15   £B
Deliciously soft, ripe bargain. Easy drinking.

Moondah Brook Cabernet Sauvignon 1991   12   £C

Normans Chandlers Hill Shiraz 1992   17   £D
Perfumed, soft, quite brilliantly accessible berried fruit which
is complex, dry and effortlessly coats the tongue with flavour.

Penfolds Bin 407 Cabernet Sauvignon 1990   16   £E
Superb specimen. Soft fruit with blackcurrant flavour in solid,
impressive form.

**Penfolds Coonawarra Cabernet Sauvignon
1990**   17   £E
The colour of crushed blackberries, subtle eucalyptus/leather
aroma, sheer-satiny acids and velvet-textured fruit touches –
lovely tannicky finish.

Rockford Grenache 1991   15   £D
Delicious, slightly minty wine. Very soft.

Vasse Felix Cabernet Sauvignon 1987   10   £F

AUSTRALIAN WINE – *white*

Cape Mentelle Chardonnay 1989   13   £E
Over the hill just a touch now.

Denham Estate Semillon 1993   13   £B

Normans South Australia Chenin Blanc 1992   14   £D
Interesting and tasty.

Penfolds Bin 21 Chardonnay 1993   14   £C
Delicious ripe, balanced fruit and comely acids.

Penfolds Bin 202 South Australian Riesling n.v.   13   £C
An attractive, interesting wine.

Rosemount Chardonnay 1993   15   £D
Elegant, oily fruit. Superb.

Wakefield Crouchen Chardonnay 1989   16   £C
Terrific toasty 'come-on' aroma. Deep flavour, lengthy finish.
Great vigour and force here.

Yates Original Australian White Wine n.v.   11   £D
Pour it over ice-cream.

Yeringberg Lily Marsanne 1987   13   £F
Interesting curiosity for deeply committed wine buffs.

BULGARIAN WINE – *red*

Bulgarian Cabernet/Mavrud 1989   14   £B

CHILEAN WINE – *red*

Cousino Macul Antiguas Reservas 1989	14	£C
Portal del Alto Cabernet Sauvignon 1992	14	£C

CHILEAN WINE – *white*

Cousino Macul Chardonnay 1992	13	£C

FRENCH WINE – *red*

Abbaye St-Hilaire, Coteaux Varois 1992   16 £B
Excellent value. Dryness and real frutiness, softness yet no yukkiness. Savoury, rich, balanced superbly.

Bergerac Rouge (Booths) n.v.   12 £B

Booths Claret n.v.   12 £B

Booths Vin Rouge n.v.   12 £B

Bourgogne Hautes-Côtes de Beaune Red 1990   12 £D

Cabernet Sauvignon, Ardéche 1992   15 £B
Some real 'green' touches to the fruit here. Great food wine (roast food).

Cahors, Côtes d'Olt 1989   15 £B
Brilliant softness and yielding plummy fruit. Perfect maturity at a bargain price.

Château Dolibey 1990   11 £C

Château Laval Costières de Nîmes 1992   13 £B
Sweet finish to fruit of some style.

Château Ollieux, Corbières 1991   14 £C
Soft and cuddly.

Château Pierrail Bordeaux 1990   13 £C
Excellent fruit and softly developing tannins.

Côtes de Beaune Villages 1991   11 £C

Côtes du Rhône 1990 (Booths)   14 £B
Good value here.

Crozes-Hermitage Mousset 1991   11 £C

**Domaine de la Grande Courtade, Vin de Pays de
l'Herault 1992**   14 £B
Rich fruit, attractive tannins.

Fleurie La Madone 1991   14 £D
Perfect maturity – savoury, rich, a trooper of a seasoned
beaujolais.

Mas de Daumas Gassac Rouge 1988   15 £F
Ready now.

Mas de Daumas Gassac Rouge 1990   16 £F
Very good wine now. Brilliant and possibly 18–19 points in
three to four years.

Michel Lynch Bordeaux Rouge 1990   12 £E
An overrated wine of some charm in the middle, but little
effective structure either side. Very expensive for the paucity
of style on offer.

Rasteau, Domaine la Soumade 1990 15 £D
Superb wine with soft berried fruits and a suede quality to the tannin. Good now, in a couple of years it'll rate 17–18.

St-Maurice Côtes du Rhône Villages 1992 14 £C
Good fruit, good structure, good price.

St-Pourcain Rouge Domaine de la Croix d'Or 1992 12 £C

Vosne Romanée Cacheux 1990 12 £G
This has some pleasant fruit with smoky edges, but with a price to pay.

FRENCH WINE – *white*

Bergerac Blanc (Booths) n.v. 11 £B

Booths Vin Blanc n.v. 14 £B
Terrific value for the genuineness of the fruit on offer.

Bordeaux Blanc 1992 (Booths) 11 £B

Bordeaux Blanc Sec (Medium Dry) n.v. 12 £B

Bourgogne Aligote, Buxy n.v. 14 £C
Attractive level of richness here.

Chablis Paul Grimaudet 1992 12 £C

Chardonnay Vin de Pays des Côteaux Baronnies 1992 15 £B
Great value – smells like a white burgundy, finishes like a Côtes du Rhône blanc.

Château de Passan Blanc 1992   14   £C
Elegant, demure, purposeful.

Château Haut-Rian Blanc Sec 1992   14   £C
Good weight of fruit. Stylish.

Château Pierrail White 1992   13   £C

Côtes Bergerac Blanc (Booths) n.v.   10   £B

Graves Blanc Oak Aged 1991   16   £C
Dotty French label with a maritime theme. Ignore this and
concentrate on the superbly supple fruit in the wine.

James Herrick Chardonnay 1992   15   £C
Delicious, almost New World buttery fruit.

Mersault H. Gaboureau 1989   11   £E

Muscadet Sur Lie Livraudier 1992   14   £C
One of the better muscadets I've tasted.

Muscat Cuvée José Sala n.v.   15   £C
Toffee nosed and less than £4? Aristocratic sweetness never
came so cheap.

Pinot Blanc Turkheim 1992   14   £C
Fruit edging towards the ripe – excellent aperitif.

GERMAN WINE – *white*

Booths Hock n.v.   13   £A
As good as any liebfraumilch on the market at half the price.

Booths Liebfraumilch n.v.   12   £B

L' Philipp Bacchus 1991	11	£C
L' Philipp Müller-Thurgau n.v.	11	£C

Louis Guntrum Oppenheimer Sack Gewürztraminer Auslese n.v. 14 £E
An aperitif to stun your friends and astonish your neighbours.

Oppenheimer Herrenberg Silvaner Kabinett 1990 14 £C
Delicious aperitif.

Robert Weil Riesling Kabinett 1990	13	£D

ITALIAN WINE – *red*

Chianti Classico, Contessa Di Radda 1988	14	£D
Chianti Classico del Macia 1991	13	£C
Chianti Classico Riservadi Fizzano 1988	13	£E
Chianti Rialto 1992	11	£B

Lambrusco Grasparossa di Castevetro n.v. 13 £B
The real thing. Try it with cold meats.

Rialto Sangiovese n.v. (2 litres) 11 £D
A large bottle with a screw top.

Teroldego Rotaliano 1992	12	£C

ITALIAN WINE – *white*

Bianco di Custoza Rizzi 1992   12   £D

Bottichio Rosso n.v.   12   £B

LEBANESE WINE – *white*

Château Musar White 1989   10   £D
Stick to red wine-making, Gaston.

NEW ZEALAND WINE – *white*

Cook's Chardonnay/Chenin Blanc 1992   13   £C

Cook's Riesling/Chenin Blanc 1992   11   £C

PORTUGUESE WINE – *red*

Booths Crusted 1989 Bottled Port   16   £E
So much flavour at half the price of a comparable vintage port.

Niepoort LBV 1987 Bottled Port   15   £E
Very attractive, deep fruit.

Niepoort Ruby Port n.v.   14   £D
Lots of character for a ruby.

Quinta de la Rosa Red 1992   13   £C

SOUTH AFRICAN WINE – *red*

Clear Mountain Pinotage n.v.   13   £B

SOUTH AFRICAN WINE – *white*

Charles Gerard Reserve, Fairview Estate 1990 13   £C

Charles Gerard Reserve White 1991   15   £C
At its peak of quiet authority.

Clear Mountain Chenin Blanc n.v.   14   £B
Layered fruit here, agreeably complex for the money.

Eersterivière Chardonnay 1990   12   £C
Getting tired and a mite flabby around the edges, but excellent with grilled chicken.

Two Oceans White 1993   10   £C

SPANISH WINE – *red*

Cune Rioja Crianza 1990   14   £C

Cune Rioja Reserva 1987   16   £D
Gorgeous.

Gran Condal Rioja Red 1992   14   £B

Ochoa Navarra Red Tinto 1991   14 £C
Ripe, flavoursome, persistent. Has vanillary undertones.

Ochoa Tempranillo 1990   16 £D
Superb fruit. As friendly as a fruitgum, as complex as a
grandiose Bordeaux.

Viñas de Gain Rioja Red 1990   15 £C

SPANISH WINE – *white*

Booths Amontillado Medium Sherry   14 £C
Also available in litre bottles at £5.29.

Booths Fino Sherry   15 £C
Perfect example. Also available in litre bottles at £5.29.

Booths Manzanilla Sherry   16 £C
Camomile and saline nuts. Brilliant.

Carraixet. Moscatel de Valencia n.v.   15 £B
Soft marmalade fruit and quince-jelly acidity. Great value.

Tizon Palo Cortado Sherry   17 £E
The unique effect of real fruit undercut by an intense dryness.
Like a cello chord struck and lingering for minutes before it
dies.

USA WINE – *white*

Glen Ellen Chardonnay 1992   15 £C
Delicious structure from start to finish – has fruit, acid, balance, style.

YUGOSLAVIAN WINE – *white*

Vranac Red 1991   12 £B

SPARKLING WINE/CHAMPAGNE

Booths Champagne Brut n.v.   14 £F

Brossault Rosé   14 £E
Worth the roses.

Cellar 5

Warrington was once famous for its wodka, but it will forever stay in my memory for Ridge Paso Robles Zinfandel 1991. The taste of this wine, the highest scoring in this book, stayed with me as I enjoyed a short walk about the town after I had gargled and spat my way through a range of Cellar 5 bottles. Such was the force of the zin's fruit, concentrated figs and cassis, that nothing, not even the shock of turning the street corner and coming upon the massive wrought-iron extravaganza, freshly licked by gold paint and topped by golden angels, of the town hall's gates, could dislodge it. Formerly the home of Lord Winmarleigh, the town hall has a certain military aspect but those gates . . . those gates could open for Britain. If you enjoy grand entrances, you must visit Warrington. Also go if you enjoy red wine (or visit one of Cellar 5's 490-odd shops in the north-east, Midlands, and North Wales).

The other side of the Manchester Ship Canal from the Town of the Golden Gate is Stockton Heath (known in Victorian times as a centre for spade manufacture). It's a prime spot for a Cellar 5 shop. As I walked around its spacious square footage a woman walked through the door, strode up to the manager Brian Walsh and, bold as brass, said: 'Excuse me, do you have any Eiswein?' Mr Walsh was stumped. I was gobsmacked. Down in the poor south we've forgotten what Eiswein – that horrendously expensive German invention made ounce by ounce from frozen overripe grapes – tastes like. Who can afford it? But Cellar 5 customers can afford to splash out on wine and the comprehensive wine list is an enormous inspiration. What would be the best-selling wine in a place like this? A smart off-licence which also sells fags, candy bars and continental ice-cream and chocolates? 'Muscadet used to be the best seller,' said Mr Walsh, 'but then the Australians got going. But the Santa Rita is probably the best-selling white wine of the week at the moment.' You mean it's outselling £2.50 sweet Germans? A £4.99 Chilean? He smiled pityingly at poor me.

A subsidiary of the Greenall Group which also runs pubs and hotels, the wine shops trade either as Cellar 5 or as the somewhat more up-market Berkeley Wines (and the wines which are only available at BW shops are so indicated in the list which follows). Whether the latter operation, on the evidence of the shop I visited, is truly up-market (competing, say, with Thresher's posher wine subsidiaries) is a very moot point. Mr Walsh may have a pseudo-antique delivery van parked out back, but this is just mobile window-dressing and as corny as those soap-powder commercials where ham actors wearing white coats attempt to pass themselves off as scientists. At least Mr Walsh himself is mercifully free from any pretensions and not dolled up in a striped three-piece suit with a gold fob watch. A Berkeley Wine shop is surely just a flash offy stocking more expensive wines than a Cellar 5 shop. Two minutes after the woman looking for Eiswein left disappointed (buying instead an excellent bottle of the honeyed Ste Croix-du-Mont) a customer came in and asked for a packet of Woodbines. I itched to suggest the Ridge Zinfandel (having spotted half-a-dozen bottles on a top shelf); more expensive, but much healthier than any Woodbine.

Cellar 5 is the third largest off-licence chain in the UK, behind Victoria Wine and Thresher, but in its heartland it competes strongly. It was to strengthen this competitiveness that the company hired a new managing director in April, previously operations director at Thresher. At the time of writing, however, there is no wine buyer. Gerard Barnes, who held the job until spring this year, packed his bags and took off to become bordeaux, burgundy and beaujolais buyer for Sainsbury's. I suspect that his job will be filled by two buyers, possibly one of either sex.

I spoke to Ian Bryden, marketing manager, and he said it was 'an interesting time from our point of view'. He went on to explain. 'I think that the public will see a significant change in the direction of the Cellar 5 group of companies. We're looking at the whole aspect of segmentation. We're moving towards a situation where we will have a wine specialist company, approximately thirty shops, at the very top end of the wine market.'

Not called Cellar 5 or Berkeley Wines?

'No. The name has yet to be decided. We will also introduce more Berkeley Wines stores by converting existing Cellar 5s. About 150. The balance of stores will be divided between the convenience type, where there'll be an element of food, and the remainder will be Cellar 5 stores, primarily off-licences. There's an enormous amount of work being done in redefining the range and the shop appearance, the layout and the shelving, and we're at the stage where we're just bringing it all together.'

As I see it, the reason for the new trend towards up-market wine shops is because the supermarkets have pinched so much of the off-licence chains' traditional business. The upper end is the only place to go. But does this represent commercial logic? Mr Bryden believes it does:

'We've got some very strong sites. Over the years we've been relatively conservative in the way that we've used them. We've tended to remain with some of our off-licence base, even with our premier stores. We have been a little nervous about clearly positioning ourselves in the past. Now we want to be totally clear. There is a strong market at the top end. But whichever sector you're in, the supermarkets are competition. They're getting increasingly excellent in the way they buy, the way they merchandise. Their hours are getting longer and they're becoming awfully convenient, something we always used to be able to claim was a property for ourselves.'

What about staff training? Even the supermarkets are training their staff to understand wine better, so don't wine shops have to have even more capable, knowledgeable staff?

'We see training and education as a fundamental area. We've got to address it. All our staff are encouraged to go on the various wine-education courses. And we believe we've got to tackle it from the grass roots and make sure that whoever is on duty at the branch at whatever time when a customer comes in should be able to advise the customer and give relevant informative help, to allow them to make their choice. We see that as a major priority – to educate, train our staff and also to make the shops themselves better in terms of information on the shelf. It's an area we've been neglectful of in the past. We've just taken on a training manager to address all these issues. Wine has become a very competitive business and if we don't do our job right, the consumer has every right to choose not to trade with us. It's a big world and there's so much choice now.'

So wine writers will at last begin to hear of you? You haven't exactly courted the species, have you?

'No, we haven't. We've done the reverse of courting people like you. But there's a complete reorientation of thinking and we're now going to be very active. We'll be talking to wine writers to try to get a really strong profile within the industry.'

Cellar 5 should have no problem with wine writers if they handle them right. Just whisk 'em up to Warrington, hand out glasses of that zinfandel, and sit 'em down by the town hall gates.

AUSTRALIAN WINE – *red*

Lightning Ridge Shiraz n.v.   13   £C
Mild, spicy and soft.

Penfolds Bin 407 Cabernet Sauvignon 1990   16   £E
Superb specimen. Soft fruit with blackcurrant flavour in solid,
impressive form.

Wolf Blass Shiraz/Cabernet Sauvignon 1992   15.5   £D
The usual Blass Blast of Bruised Fruit. Lovely roast-meat
wine.

**Wolf Blass Yellow Label Cabernet Sauvignon
1992**   15.5   £D
Ripe fruit, very giving, with minty undertones. Very opulent.
Incredibly soft and velvety.

AUSTRALIAN WINE – *white*

Lightning Ridge Semillon 1993   13   £C
A pleasant aperitif.

Lindemans Bin 65 Chardonnay 1993   16   £C
Deep, bruised fruit – lovely and ripe. Superb effect on the tongue.

Mitchelton Reserve Chardonnay 1991   16   £D
The wine-maker reckons nectarines and chestnuts, and he's
right. I reckon this calls for food: salmon, chicken, fish soup.

Penfolds Semillon/Chardonnay 1993   14   £C
Excellent recipe: fruit, acid, wood, but will integrate and
improve mightily over the next one to two years.

Wolf Blass South Australian Chardonnay
1993 15.5 £D
Gorgeous toasty aromas and buttery fruit, finishing with a tang. Great with gentle fish curries and grilled chicken.

BULGARIAN WINE – *red*

Lyaskovets Reserve Merlot 1985 15 £C
A bargain for the mature-fruit lover who likes a plumper figure. A touch figgy – even a bit raisiny. Late-middle-aged, certainly. Good with food – cheese and chat a sound bet with it. Only available in Berkeley Wine stores.

Oriachovitsa Reserve Merlot/Cabernet Sauvignon
1989 15 £B
Great value fruit of purpose and style.

BULGARIAN WINE – *white*

Khan Krum Reserve Chardonnay/Sauvignon
Blanc 1990 14 £B
Good chewy quality to ripe, mature fruit. Excellent with rich fish dishes.

CHILEAN WINE – *red*

Santa Carolina Cabernet Sauvignon 1992   16   £C
Very elegant and almost lazy. Seems effortless in its black-currantiness, which has a sweet polish to the finish. Excellent value.

Santa Carolina Cabernet Sauvignon/Merlot
1992   16   £C
Combines the multi-dimensional virtues of both cabernet and merlot, and yet in losing the identity of each in the blend, an added length of flavour is acquired.

CHILEAN WINE – *white*

Santa Carolina Chardonnay 1992   15   £C
Subtly toffeed fruit lurking behind a woody flavouring of gentility but presence. Very, very elegant.

Santa Carolina Sauvignon Blanc 1993   15   £C
Brilliant value. Has lovely, richly endowed fruit with length and elegance. A great bottle to enjoy solo: has complexity.

Santa Rita Sauvignon Blanc Reserve 1993   15   £C
Lush strata of flavour under soothing acidity. Delicious. Only available in Berkeley Wine stores.

FRENCH WINE – *red*

Beaujolais Villages Les Vaudières 1992   11 £C
Pleasant. Expensive.

Beaumes de Venise Cuvée D. Tocque 1991   16 £C
Bitingly deep, rich fruit. Dry, refined, full, almost opulent. A
superb, individual Côtes du Rhône for roast meats or game.

Château Canet, Minervois 1991   16 £B
Brilliant drinking. Plums, black cherries and cherries in a
fruity medley which finishes drily. This is a terrific bottle for
the money.

Château Haut-Marbuzet 1988   17 £F
Lovely cigar-box aroma. Glorious mature fruit with the tannins holding it up thrillingly. Pricey, but truly a class act of
verve, style and hypnotic flavouring.

Château le Redon, Bordeaux 1990   13 £C
Sweet, then rather overwhelmingly dry, this is a softly fruited,
attractive wine.

Château Mandourelle, Corbières 1991   13.5 £B
Very good value. Drying out on the finish, the fruit, but
otherwise very soundly made.

Claret Duboscq n.v.   13.5 £C
Superb introduction to serious claret for the beginner. Excellent style of fruit, and a hint of tannins. Well made.

Crozes-Hermitage Chonion 1991   13 £D
Tasty. A touch pricey for the taste, but the taste is there.

FRENCH WINE – *white*

Chardonnay Domaine de Lissac, Vin de Pays d'Oc
1992   12   £C
Not bad fruit, even some varietal purity.

Château des Coulinats, Ste Croix-du-Mont
1988   15   £E
A woody, honeyed wine with richly riveting fruit in the Monbazillac mould.

Côtes de Gascogne Domaine Maison 1992   10   £C
I would say this was made from grapes grown in that part of
the vineyard which received little sun. Only available in
Berkeley Wine stores.

Domaine Fontanelles Sauvignon Blanc 1993   14   £C
Gooseberries and gentle lemons: a good combination of fruit,
with elegance and weight, for fish and shellfish. Good price.
Only available in Berkeley Wine stores.

Les Hauterigues, Sancerre 1992   8   £D
The least attractive sancerre I've touched in ages.

Premier Côtes de Bordeaux   12   £D
Some attractive, slightly honeyed fruit. Pud wine? Yes, but
very light pud.

Sauvignon de St-Bris Broccard 1992   11   £D

GERMAN WINE – *white*

Graacher Himmelreich 1993   11   £C
Probably better when the century's turned.

Liebfraumilch Cellar 5 1992   12   £B
About as friendly as this much despised genre can get.

Oppenheimer Krotenbrunnen 1992   13   £C
One glass of this would be a pleasant aperitif.

Wehlener Sonnenhur 1991   12   £C
Some lemonic presence to please riesling freaks, but
expensive.

HUNGARIAN WINE – *red*

**Hungarian Cabernet Sauvignon, Balaton Boglar
n.v.**   14   £B
Lots of value in this ripe, soft fruit which is berried and
delicious. Essentially dry, but lots of fruitiness.

HUNGARIAN WINE – *white*

Hungarian Cabernet Sauvignon 1991   10   £B

Hungarian Chardonnay, Balaton Boglar 1993   13   £B
Excellent shellfish wine. Has some backbone.

ITALIAN WINE – *red*

Barbera Piemonte 1993   15   £B
Terrific value here; the wine is fully structured, dry yet fruity, full
of flavour and versatile with food. Sweet, almost raspberry finish.

Trentino Cabernet 1991   14   £C
Nice, rich, black-cherry touch to the soft blackcurrant fruit.
Delicious pasta wine. Only available in Berkeley Wine stores.

Trentino Merlot 1992   15   £C
Solidly fruity and dry, but with lots of rounded plum fruit. Has
a rich, savoury edge of maturity, yet is essentially a young,
vigorously pleasing wine.

ITALIAN WINE – *white*

Trentino Chardonnay 1993   12   £C
Only available in Berkeley Wine stores.

Trentino Pinot Bianco 1993   11   £C

Trentino Pinot Grigio 1993   13   £C
Attractively fruited in a peachy/apricoty sort of way.

NEW ZEALAND WINE – *white*

Timara Dry White 1993   14   £C
Exceptionally tasty with echoes of grass, but mostly rich fruit.
Delicious appetite reviver.

PORTUGUESE WINE – *red*

Bairrada Tinto 1990   15 £C
Figs and a touch of creamy soft fruit. Ripe, mature, rich,
brilliant value. Roast food is its partner. Only available in
Berkeley Wine stores.

SOUTH AFRICAN WINE – *red*

Backsberg Klein Babylonstoren 1991   15 £D
Curiously satisfying. Woody and ripe, deep, rich and soft.

Backsberg Pinotage 1991   13.5 £C
Pulls up short but otherwise this has some flavour while it
lasts. The acidity practises *coitus interruptus* on the fruit.

SOUTH AFRICAN WINE – *white*

Backsberg Estate Chardonnay 1992   15 £D
Weight and length deceptive here – the wine appears demure
but the fruit is full and lingering. Classy.

Firgrove Chenin Blanc n.v.   13 £B
Has a soft, waxy, muted honey edge to the fruit. Good with
salads.

SPANISH WINE – *red*

Casa de la Viña 1993   15.5   £B
Lots of vividly rounded fruit; plums and blackcurrants. Dry,
soft and smooth. Brilliant value.

Casa de la Viña Reserve 1985   17   £C
Stunning value. Creamy vanilla fruit which is neither big nor
aggressive, but soothing and smooth. Perfectly mature – it has
a lovely tannic presence, without harshness, but is essentially a
strawberry ice-cream sundae made into wine. Impressive
drinking for the music lover or bookworm in no need of
human company.

Marqués D. Villamagna 1992   13   £F
Lots of fruit, lots of money. Do they balance? Not quite.

Montefiel Oaky Red n.v.   14   £B
Great with food. Ripe, rich fruit, a trifle earthy, but terrific
value for money.

Santa Maria n.v.   13   £B
Soft, squashy, raisiny fruit. Good with pasta and pizzas.

Tres Puertes, La Mancha Red n.v.   15   £B
Excellent value fruit for simple meat and vegetable dishes.

SPANISH WINE – *white*

La Mancha Blanco, Tres Puertes 1992   13   £B
Sour fruit, some breezy acidity. Fish and chips will suit it well.

Montefiel White n.v. 13 £B
Clean, muted melon fruit. Simple but attractive.

Santa Maria Dry White n.v. 12 £B
Basic fruit, not a lot of acidity but some. Passes muster as a
party wine, certainly.

USA WINE – *red*

Christian Brothers Classic Red n.v. 13 £C
Some delicious sweet-plum fruit in an essentially dry wine.

Fetzer Valley Cask Cabernet Sauvignon 1991 14 £D
Sound fruit – expensive, but sound. Tasty, soft and spicy.

Madak Ridge Ruby Cabernet n.v. 16 £B
Terrific value. Masses of flavour and fruit which never drops
below a level of real seriousness. Great for rich food as well as
cheeses.

Palmer Vineyards Cabernet Sauvignon 1988 14 £E
Grown on Long Island, this wine is not great value, but it is
very well made in a minor bordeaux style.

Ridge Paso Robles Zinfandel 1991 19 £E
A great wine. Here are rich aromas of spiced plum and
blackberry fruit of such rich-edged, soft, berried flavour that
its intensity invokes tears. Great structure to the whole performance. Magnificently seductive and fantastic value for
under a tenner. There's nothing else like it.

USA WINE – *white*

Christian Brothers Classic White n.v.   12   £C
Attractive fruit, straightforward, unfussy.

Fetzer Sundial Chardonnay 1992   11   £D
I'm sorry to sound snobbish, but this wine has a common,
sluttish sort of fruit quality to it not worthy of £6.99.

SPARKLING WINE/CHAMPAGNE

Blass Brut (Australia) n.v.   14.5   £E
Wolf Blass couldn't make a wine without fruit if you moved
the winery to the Sahara. This is no exception.

Louis Daumont Champagne n.v.   12   £F

René Florancy Blanc de Blancs n.v. (France)   13   £G

Seppelt Great Western Brut n.v. (Australia)   16   £C
Superb bargain. A finer fizzer on sale for under a fiver it's
difficult to name. Lemony, zingy, zesty. Great style.

Seppelt Great Western Rosé n.v.   15   £D

Davisons

The recession was a smack in the teeth for this century-old, seventy-seven-shop-strong, southern-based group of 'Wine Merchants and Victuallers'. 'It hit us sideways,' muttered Michael Davies, managing director, through clenched lips set in a straight-jawed face with a suggestion of a ski-tan.

Well, if you're going to be hit, then sideways is a better direction to travel than back. And as I first looked over the range of wines Mr Davies had laid out on the boardroom table for me to taste, back was certainly the directions things were pointing. Not only did walled portraits of Churchill and Lloyd George (to whom Mr Davies' grandfather, Sir Alfred Davies, was a personal secretary) observe my every sip, rather expressionlessly I thought, but the wines were from hallowed areas of France where wine producers are licensed under new *appellation contrôlée* regulations to shoot to kill any superplonker found trespassing, as freely as they are permitted to extinguish vermin. Thus I tasted five different vintages of Château Cardaillan, a red Graves (all, uncommercially in my view, eccentrically at the same price); three of Château Maucaillou, a Moulis, and three of Château Villars, a Fronsac; a couple of vintages of Santenay Clos Roussea; ditto Les Guettes Savigny-les-Beaune and Domaine Burguet Gevrey-Chambertin; and a bundle of white burgundies up to a premier cru Chassagne-Montrachet.

As you will see from the listing of these Davison wines in this book, I was taken with some of these bottles, not so taken with others. But none gave me a thrill or provided any surprises. What did provoke these reactions, however, was a Spaniard and an Australian: Muaro 1984 is the former; E & E

Black Pepper Shiraz 1991 the latter. I was delighted to find these under the very nose of Winston Churchill.

I didn't taste the whole range of wines at Davisons. No mortal could in a single day and live to tell of it. The range is vast and the printed list available at the shops gives no indication of the stock held in the cellars. This includes a selection of first, second, third, fourth and fifth-growth clarets going back to 1966 Château Haut-Brion and forward to 1988 Château La Lagune; a solid parcel of mid-80s barsacs and sauternes; some forty-odd vintage ports (Taylor, Graham, Warre, Croft, Cockburn, Dow, Sandeman, Quinta do Noval and Fonseca) from the '60 vintage on; and a number of champagnes. The shop list is also sound, offering, as well as all the wines from the areas you would expect, a decent selection from South Africa and California, and some interesting Spanish and Italian wines. Chile is perfunctory (three wines), so is Alsace. But there are ten Californians and five Romanians, and a sound selection both red and white from Australia. Australian sparkling wine is the fastest-growing sector in Davisons store with sales up 150 per cent. As a matter of record, and no little interest, Davisons record French wine sales 10 per cent down, Germany 12 per cent down and Italy 5 per cent down. South Africa shows the liveliest upward trend (45 per cent), followed by Australia (40 per cent) and California (30 per cent). France represents 38 per cent of the store's total throughput.

How have they survived through these past, potentially crippling, lean years? By the idiosyncrasy and personal determination of the shop managers, as much as by any prudent financial leadership from head office (though whether it is prudent to have every vintage of that Graves available at the same price is open to question, for where is the profit to the company in cellaring and ageing the stock?). One shop, so I was told, had a cheese counter where the manager's wife offered four dozen cheeses. Other shops do a steady trade in all sorts of the things the usual off-licence handles. These shops are run with a degree of independence. One manager, witnessing a clumsy customer leaving his shop and dropping and smashing on the pavement two bottles of highly expensive Chassagne-Montrachet bought for her father's birthday, felt sufficiently moved to replace both without additional payment. This gesture was felt by his own pocket as much as the company's, for managers earn a salary plus a percentage of controllable profits (plus a percentage of the annual increase). 'We invest in managers,' Michael Davies told me. 'Each runs a family business of his own within another family business called Davisons.' These managers are certainly well received when they come up with new ideas. It was a shop manager who came up with the idea of forty-nine days on, two weeks off for the couple (married, or partners) who run each branch and so far fifty out of the seventy-seven shops have adopted this novel idea. It is made workable by the existence of twelve permanent trainee relief-couples who come in during the usual incumbents' fortnight off. This is a tremendous fund of experience as Davisons expand, using relief couples to run their own stores as they become available. These shops vary, with the most wine-orientated doing 55 per cent wine business to a low of 15 per cent; the remaining turnover is in beer, spirits, mineral waters and soft drinks, tobacco, crisps and confectionery. The percentage of turnover attributable to wine has gone up over the past ten years, but whether this will continue is arguable with the increasing popularity of cross-Channel trading that southern boozers indulge in.

The company also runs several pubs, a wine mail-order business, and has the original Master Cellar (a name Tesco felt important enough to lease off Davisons for a range of its own wines) next to the head office in Aberdeen Road, Croydon, where, I was intrigued to record on the day I visited the place, the Indian sparkling wine Omar Khayyám was that week's top-selling tipple. Unpredictable place, Aberdeen Road, Croydon.

Perfect address for Davisons.

AUSTRALIAN WINE – *red*

Church Block Red, McLaren Vale Wirra Wirra
1991 13 £D

Craigmoor Mudgee Cabernet Sauvignon 1990 14 £D
Rich, chewy, tarry, burnt-edged, savoury fruit. Excellent roast-food wine.

E & E Black Pepper Shiraz 1991 18 £F
Commanding bouquet, sublime, ripe molar-crunching fruit with eucalyptus and liquorice undertones, and it throws in soft, chewy tannins of sufficient weight to suggest sufficient development potential, and further flavour enhancement, for five to fifteen years more. Tremendous wine – Hermitage meets Barolo. Pricey, but well priced. A magnificent testimony to the quality of fruit. Without question a product of very low-yielding vines. Great cheese wine.

Parrots Hill Barossa Cabernet Sauvignon 1992 16 £D
Delightful soft fruit with minty undertones. Firmly blackcurranty, it has oodles of flavour, yet it is never so impactful it numbs the palate for further glasses.

AUSTRALIAN WINE – *white*

Craigmoor Mudgee Chardonnay 1991   14   £D
Rich, flavourful, gentle – buttered fruit.

Penfolds Koonunga Hill Chardonnay 1992   14   £C
Full, lush fruit plus a ticklish dollop of lemon zest. Delicious,
but getting pricey near a fiver.

Penfolds Organic Chardonnay/Sauvignon Blanc
1993   16   £D
A happy marriage. Fine, rich fruit plus gentle, rolling acidity
make for a perfect balance of flavours from start to finish. Has
a very sophisticated polish to it.

AUSTRIAN WINE – *white*

Servus n.v.   10   £B

CHILEAN WINE – *red*

Caliterra Cabernet Sauvignon 1991   14   £C
Dry, lovely dry-blackcurrant fruit. Very classically moulded
and finished.

CHILEAN WINE – *white*

Caliterra Chardonnay Reserve 1992   16   £D
Ripe and very full in one sense, yet just as it seems the fruit
will topple over, the acidity slaps it into line. Superb, perfect
quaffing tipple for the well-heeled, for whom white burgundy
went the way of the parlour maid and the wing collar.

Caliterra Sauvignon Blanc 1993   16   £C
Elegant, slightly lemon fruit, classy, demure, not tough.
Lovely clear aperitif wine. Excellent structure.

FRENCH WINE – *red*

**Chambolle Musigny, Les Nazoines, Domaine
Machard de Gramont 1988**   11   £G

Château Cardaillan, Graves 1985   16   £D
Superb, perfect mature claret of impressive weight of fruit,
soft tannins and fine acidic balance. A beauty. And a rare one
under £7.

Château Cardaillan, Graves 1986   15   £D
As above, but not so fiercely classy and full.

Château Cardaillan, Graves 1988   13   £D

Château Cardaillan, Graves 1989   13   £D

Château Cardaillan, Graves 1990   13   £D

Château de Barbe, Côtes de Bourg 1990   13   £D
Almost 14 points, but not quite – quiet on the finish.

Château Maucaillou, Moulis 1986   13   £F

Château Maucaillou, Moulis 1989   14   £F
Complex clump of fruit on the palate. Will age extremely
interestingly.

Château Maucaillou, Moulis 1990   14   £F
More vegetal characteristics in this vintage.

Château Mendoce, Côtes de Bourg 1990   14   £D
Highly attractive, soft in its tannins and blackcurrant fruit.
Stylish. Good value.

Château Villars, Fronsac 1986   16   £E
Lovely. Blackcurrant fruit with typical suede edges to it. Classy,
deep, flavourful.

Château Villars, Fronsac 1988   14   £E

Château Villars, Fronsac 1989   13   £E

Châteauneuf-du-Pape, Font de Michelle 1989   13   £F

Châteauneuf-du-Pape, Font de Michelle 1990   15   £F
Superb wine of a superb year: rich, deep, complex (fruit offers
soft berries and herbs and a bunch of violets) and lovely to drink
with both rich food and rich conversation.

**Gevrey-Chambertin, Vieilles Vignes, Domaine
Burguet 1989**   13   £G
Delicious. Rotten value, but delicious. Has rich, savoury fruit
of some decisiveness, but lacks the complexity a £20 wine must
have.

**Gevrey-Chambertin, Vieilles Vignes, Domaine
Burguet 1990**   12   £G
Hasn't the weight of the above but in ten years might be very
interesting indeed. But I'd rather put my £20 on a horse.

Michel Lynch Bordeaux Rouge 1990   12   £E
An overrated wine of some charm in the middle, but little
effective structure either side. Very expensive for the paucity
of style on offer.

Moulin à Vent, Domaine Tour de Bief Duboeuf
1992   11   £E

Red Rhône and French Country Wine n.v.   13   £C
Some soft, burnt fruit here.

Santenay Clos Rousseau, Domaine Morey 1989   12   £G

Santenay Clos Rousseau, Domaine Morey 1990   11   £G

Santenay, Le Chainey Domaine Morey 1987   12   £F
Nice wild-strawberry touches to the fruit, but falling down at
the finish.

Savigny Les Beaune Les Guettes Domaine
Pavelot 1989   10   £G

Savigny Les Beaune Les Guettes Domaine
Pavelot 1990   13   £G
Some burgundian pinot-noir character showing here. But it's
still like seeing the play from the back of the theatre.

Savigny Les Beaunes Les Guettes Domaine
Pavelot 1988   10   £G

FRENCH WINE – *white*

Bourgogne Aligote Bouzeron, Ancien Domaine
Carnot 1992   12   £D

**Chassagne-Montrachet Premier Cru, Les
Chaumées Domaine**   14   £H
It is a superb white wine. But then at £25 it should be.

Château de Sours Blanc 1992   14   £D
Gentle gaminess behind the soft melon fruit. Classy.
Delicious.

**James Herrick Chardonnay, Vin de Pays d'Oc
1993**   14   £C
Some attractive richness here.

M. de Malle, Graves 1991   14   £E
This is a good, well-built wine, but it is expensive. Varietally
very faithful.

Meursault Les Cloux, Domaine Javillier 1989   14   £G
Stylish aromatically, but the finish lets down the rest of the
production. Especially at £15.

Meursault Les Cloux, Domaine Javillier 1990   13   £G

**Pouilly Blanc Fumé AC Domaine André
Chatelain 1992**   13   £E

**Sauvignon de Touraine AC Domaine des Sablons
1992**   15   £C
Tight gooseberry fruit, grassy supports. Delicious shellfish
wine.

**Sauvignon Trois Moulins, Vine de Pays d'Oc
1992**   14   £C
Excellent varietal character.

**St-Aubin, Les Charmois Premier Cru, Domaine
Morey 1990**   13   £G

St-Romain, Clossou le Château Jean Germain
1991   15   £F
An impressive minor white burgundy. It has maturity and
balance, an old-fashioned style of fruit, and is very sure of
itself. All is not lost in Burgundy with minor appellations so
classy, but why must it cost over a tenner?

GERMAN WINE – *white*

Bernkasteler Lay Riesling Kabinett, S.A.Prum   14   £E
Brilliant sherbet-lime aroma with racing acidic fruit, laced
with lemon. Classy aperitif.

Oppenheimer Sacktrager, Silvaner Kabinett
Halbtrocken n.v.   13   £E

ITALIAN WINE – *red*

Barbera d'Alba, Prunotto Pian Romualdo 1990   11   £E
I was looking forward to experiencing this wine's full embrace
and was merely kissed, politely, on the cheek.

Merlot del Veneto, Via Nova 1992   12   £B

ITALIAN WINE – *white*

Chardonnay del Friuli Villa del Borgo 1993   14   £C
Stylish, clean, some attractive prickly acid to the gentle fruit.

Nuragus di Cagliari, Sardinia, Dolia 1992   15   £C
Lovely strawberry/raspberry fruit showing through the crisp
acid. Has a deliciousness of surprising complexity.

SOUTH AFRICAN WINE – *white*

Cape Cellars Sauvignon Blanc 1992   14   £C
Modern, fruity, clean grapey flavours with pear-drop undertones. Excellent value.

Dieu Donne Chardonnay 1993   15   £E
Faint echoes of lemon to the woody fruit make this an
appealing bottle. Some classiness on show, and style, and with
more bottle age might become truly outstanding.

SPANISH WINE – *red*

Don Giulias Tinto n.v.   16   £B
Soft, compelling fruit with tons of flavour and gentle vanillary
underneath. Plump, ripe wine of terrific drinkability. Exceptional value.

Laturce Rioja 1992   15   £C
Superb new-style rioja. Agreeable, gentle, berried fruit,
admirably structured. Good value.

Mauro, Bodegas Mauro Tudela de Duero 1984   15   £E
Big, jammy wine of some heft. Curiously like a northern
Rhône in some respects, it also resembles zinfandel and
South Australian shiraz. Expensive treat for cold winter
nights.

SPARKLING WINE/CHAMPAGNE

Champagne Charles Ellner 1986   16   £G
Delicious digestive-biscuit aroma. Touch of croissant
richness on the fruit. But considering this level of complexity,
not a lot of bread where it matters most.

Fullers

How delightful to have your office cheek-by-jowl twixt a brewery and a pleasant stretch of the River Thames. How uplifting to look out and see the oldest wisteria in the United Kingdom. Such is the happy position of Fullers' new wine buyer Roger Higgs. Small wonder Mr Higgs, who looks like Clark Kent but without the flamboyant undersuit, was persuaded to leave Oddbins. He has been at the southern-based wine-store chain (and subsidiary of the London brewers) only for a matter of months, the previous incumbent having left to go to Harrods.

'I was very happy at Oddbins,' he says, 'and they taught me a lot, but though my portfolio was interesting it didn't include Chile, or South Africa, or places that I personally thought there was room to expand. All those exciting areas!'

I looked out at the view. You can't actually see the river but you can smell the brewery.

'I went to Manchester Polytechnic,' he revealed, 'and as a holiday job I stacked shelves for Oddbins and the next thing I knew I was full time. I was a very lonely manager in a very lonely shop in the north-west, and a job came up for an assistant buyer.' Five years on and he's got a listed wisteria on the Chiswick littoral and drives a Rover with a walnut fascia. I asked him, not entirely seriously, if he got the job because he performed well at a blind tasting and he gave me a totally serious answer.

'Fullers' wine director gave every candidate on the shortlist a blind tasting. He handed me a glass and said "What's that? What's it worth?" and I said "New World Chardonnay, £4.99", which is what it was.'

But what about a blind sampling the other way? Did he know what he was walking into? What does he think of Fullers wine shops?

'I've seen probably 80 per cent of the shops now. They are categorized gold, silver and bronze. The bronzes are basically beer-and-fag shops, and they won't survive the next few years when the leases come up because there's no future in that trade.

'The gold shops, about forty, they're serious wine merchants. They sell quite a lot of traditional things like vintage port, claret, burgundy, but they also have the big expanders like everywhere else, the New World, Australia – they sell a good quantity of decent wine. The silvers are somewhere in between the beer-and-fag shops and the serious wine merchants. You go to Richmond and look at what the guy there's doing. He's very keen and very enthusiastic, he does tastings and everything. My major project is to get the silver shops up to that level.'

How did he think Fullers would change with a Higgs now buying the wine?

'They'll become more informative. The staff are incredibly enthusiastic, but their knowledge level is not where Oddbins' is by any means. They're as good as if not better than anybody else, but they're not as good as Oddbins. And I think that is something that the customer will demand more and more. I mean, why otherwise would you go to a wine specialist? Tastings are obviously something that will increase dramatically at Fullers, not only for the staff but for the customers at weekends. It creates loyalty. If you're going into a shop to spend £4 on a wine, it's expensive if you don't like it.'

Did he think his customers patronized places like Oddbins as well?

'If they go somewhere else they don't go to another

specialist. I think they go to a supermarket. It's a choice between the specialist and the convenience factor. I know that from previous qualitative research. Customers were asked "Where do you go if you don't go to Oddbins?" and every time they said "Sainsbury's or Tesco".'

So is Fullers in a straight fight with the supermarkets or other wine shops?

'We can't offer what the supermarkets offer. But what we can do is sit down and spend time with wine-makers who are prepared to listen and say, "This is what you're up against. This is the £2.99 benchmark. If you can make something better than that and I can retail it at £2.99, away you go." But what you can't do is what the supermarkets will do which is to say, "I will guarantee you this volume". I've got to say to the guy, "Bend over backwards, give me everything I want and if I don't like it, tough."'

I asked him if this meant he'll develop connections in South Africa and eastern Europe – places of great weakness in the traditional lists, but increasingly the places where bargain bottles are coming from.

'Eastern Europe is difficult. It's an areas with lots of potential, but I think it's going to be another couple of years before they get it dead right. We sell wines like the Gyongyos, but they're not exciting. They're correctly vinified – fine. But there's got to be a stage two to the flying wine-maker thing. If you take an area where most of the wines are incorrectly made, or not very good, and turn them all into correct wines, that is a vast improvement but it's not exciting. You've got to move on from there. People talk about the sameness of wines because of these flying wine-makers and while that's not a problem if everything's correct and drinkable, what do you do then? They've got to make wines that represent the area they come from.'

Didn't he think Spain was interesting from that point of view? It didn't matter who made the wines, somehow they all exhibited regional typicity and local style. Mr Higgs became excited and agreed that Spain was the biggest sleeping giant in the wine world.

'That was the thing that I did with Oddbins. I was quite proud when we were made Spanish Specialist of the Year. They've got a wine at the moment, you've got to try it. It's a £3.99 garnacha from Navarra – from Bodegas Las Campañas. It was made like this: I took an American bottle to Spain and said, "This is a grenache from California. Very simply vinified. No oak. It's £6. I know you've got really good garnacha fruit in your vineyards cos we've seen it. Go and make a wine like this." And they came back with a £3.99, spicy, peppery garnacha. You must have tasted it. It's just great.'

Mr Higgs, I have tasted it. It is a terrific wine with exceptionally rich fruit for the money. If this is what Fullers' customers are in for, they're in for a treat.

AUSTRALIAN WINE – *red*

Berri Estates Cabernet Shiraz 1992   15 £C
Sweet finish to the dry fruit. Balanced full (yet not overblown), perfect style of fruit for all manner of grilled meats.

Leeton Downs Shiraz Grenache 1993   10 £C
Sweet fruit.

Penfolds Bin 35 Shiraz Cabernet 1992.   15 £C
Ripe, soft fruit with some development ahead of it. Attractive berry flavours, well-structured and balanced. Very drinkable now but a 17–18-pointer in three to four years.

Wirra Wirra RSW Shiraz 1992   13   £E
Expensively bought deliciousness which is not hugely complex, but is undeniably an enriching experience.

Wirra Wirra The Angelus 1992   15   £E
Expensive but impressive, and you can take all day and all night to drink it. Such is the power of the soft tannins.

AUSTRALIAN WINE – *white*

Leeton Downs Semillon 1993   14   £C
Mild-mannered Aussie, combining freshness with force. Delightful fruit.

Penfolds Bin 21 Semillon/Chardonnay 1993   15   £C
Fresh and lively, yet a dollop of pineappley melon keeps intruding. Delicious, refreshing wine.

Penfolds South Australia Chardonnay 1992   16   £D
Lovely polished, lush, woody fruit with touches of lemon, beautifully balanced. Elegant – a real alternative, at a far lower price, to fine burgundy.

Rockford Eden Valley Riesling 1992   13   £E
Delicious aperitif. Expensive.

**Rockford Local Growers Barossa Valley Semillon
1990**   15   £E
Grilled chicken's perfect partner: rich, toasty, melony, suggestion of peach, ripe, dry, oily and gently exotic. Lush stuff.

Tasmanian Estate Chardonnay 1992   12   £E
Oddly delicious but oddly expensive. Will perplex most drinkers except curiosity hunters.

Wirra Wirra Chardonnay 1992   14   £E
Impressively pricey.

Wirra Wirra Church Block Dry White 1993   13   £D

CHILEAN WINE – *red*

Cono Sur Cabernet Sauvignon 1993   14   £C
Dry and richly edged with a chewy quality to the fruit.

Cono Sur Pinot Noir 1993   13   £C

Cono Sur Reserve Cabernet 1992   14   £D

Torconal Merlot n.v.   15   £B
Finishes with a touch of chocolate. Superb value fruit.

FRENCH WINE – *red*

Château de Roquenagade, Corbières 1991   14   £C
Rich and well balanced. Will improve over the next two years
if cellared.

Château Gazin, Pomerol 1988   13   £G

Château La Becade, Listrac 1990   15   £D
Lovely tannins here. Bristles with serious fruit.

Château Lynch Moussas, Paullac 1990   14   £E

Château Talbot, St-Julien 1986   12   £G

Côtes du Rhône Jean Luc Colombo 1993   12   £D

Côtes du Ventoux Syrah Domaine Castellas
1990   13   £C
Fruity and simple.

Côtes Rotie Gilles Barge n.v.   10   £G
Do they stick ham bones in the barrels? Tastes like it.

Domaine de Roquenagade Cabernet Sauvignon
1991   14   £D
Deliciously dry, soft, well-balanced tannins still opening out.
Blackcurrant fruit of some weight and style.

Domaine de Sours, Bordeaux 1990   13   £D

Gevrey-Chambertin Premier Cru Les Champeaux
1991   11   £G

Grenache, Fortant de France 1993   15   £B
Rustic richness of a near opulent variety. Very attractively
balanced. Delicious to drink by itself. Hums with herby fruit.

Nuits St-Georges Premier Cru Les Vergers
1990   12   £G

FRENCH WINE – *white*

Berticot Sauvignon Blanc, Côtes de Duras
1993   15.5 £B
Great value, great style. Fresh fruit, clean as a nun's habit to
finish. Lovely balance. Very good fish wine.

Chablis Premier Cru Montmains Vauroux
n.v.   14.5 £E
Having drunk this in Chiswick Park for a Fathers' Day picnic,

I can personally testify to the wine's suitability with green grass, sunshine and outdoor food. Expensive, but very well made and true to its origins.

Chablis Vauroux 1992 15 £D
Delicious grilled-fish wine. Has elegant fruit under a mineral shroud, which is kept in check by a flinty acidity.

Coteaux de Saumur Château Hureau 1990 16 £E
No, it isn't cheap but neither is the fruit. It has the unique chenin, dry-honey fruit with a wonderful floral, honey edge to the finish. A very unusual, peachy and deeply compelling aperitif, or a wine to drink solo.

James Herrick Chardonnay 1993 14 £C
A lot has been said by the wine press on behalf of this wine. 14 says it all for me.

La Serre Chardonnay 1993 15 £C
Lovely fruit edging towards fullness but, deliciously, just hanging back. Great dashing style.

La Serre Sauvignon 1993 16 £C
Very French and concentrated enough to be as impressive, in its own way, as New Zealand sauvignon blancs. Hasn't a shred of the herbaceousness but is so pure and fresh as to be uplifting. Beautiful little wine.

Mâcon Ige Les Roches 1992 15 £C
Brilliant nutty undertones to quietly impressive fruit make this a delicious burgundy of style and representative typicity. Good price.

Mâcon-Villages Charles Vienot 1993 14 £C
Fuller (no pun intended) than the excellent Les Roches Mâcon, this has less compensating freshness of acidity and balance. Nevertheless, it is a good bottle.

ITALIAN WINES – *red*

Chianti Reserva, Villa Antinori 1989   14   £D
Demure, reluctant, aristocratic.

Teroldego Rotaliano 1991   15   £C
Chewy quality to it, yet it's squashy fruit, very ripe and dry to
finish. Has a lush, earthy undertone.

NEW ZEALAND WINES – *white*

Dashwood Marlborough Chardonnay 1992   15   £C
An admirable bottle, well priced. It offers a very attractive
combination of rich-edged, woody fruit with a pleasant fatness
to it without being gross, and the acidity is sanely citric
without shrieking. A handsomely balanced wine of no little
style.

Dashwood Sauvignon 1993   17   £E
Exquisite length of fruit on this wine. If you fail to clean your
teeth the night before, you will still taste it the next morning.
Soft melon and ripe, clean gooseberries. Brilliant wine.

Goldwater Marlborough Chardonnay 1992   15   £E
Lovely integrated wood and fruit. Textbook marriage.

Grove Hill Marlborough Sauvignon 1992   18   £E
Asparagus and celery, gooseberries and wild strawberries all
smothered in a vivacity of acidic balance which is divine.
Crisply ravishing bottle of complex fruit. Screams with
flavour. Good value for seven-and-a-half quid!!

Hunters Sauvignon Blanc 1993   15   £E
Balanced, sane, very pure and clean. Preaches fruit without screaming it.

Kumen River Chardonnay 1993   13   £G

Nobilo Marlborough Sauvignon 1993   16   £C
Impressive grassy overtones to concentrated gooseberry fruit, with a faint flicker of honey on the dry finish.

Vavasour Reserve Chardonnay 1993   12   £F

PORTUGUESE WINE – *red*

J. P. Tinto n.v.   15   £B
Light but quite delicious and fruity, without a trace of tannic harshness, oxidation or sourness. Has a plum quality to it. A true quaffing masterpiece.

PORTUGUESE WINE – *white*

J. P. Branco n.v.   14   £B
Terrific price for a terrific style of fruit. Lots of freshness and a fair dollop of flavour. Great fish wine.

João Pires Dry Moscato 1992   16   £C
Gentle muscat fruit, floral undertones. Delicious aperitif or try with fried scallops with minted-pea purée.

SOUTH AFRICAN WINE – *red*

Dieu Donne Cabernet 1992   15   £D
Mint and herbs on the delicious tannins give the blackcurrant
fruit a real lift.

Saxenburg Merlot, Stellenbosch 1992   12   £D
Touch too sweet, perhaps?

SOUTH AFRICAN WINE – *white*

Dieu Donne Chardonnay 1993   15   £D
Faint echoes of lemon to the woody fruit make this an
appealing bottle. Some classiness on show, and style, and with
more bottle age might become truly outstanding.

SPANISH WINE – *red*

Augustus Cabernet Sauvignon, Puig & Roca
1991   8   £D
Sulphur!! But that's just the bottle I tasted.

Palacio de la Vega Tempranillo, Navarra 1991   14   £D
Savoury touches to the ripe fruit which has a freshly turned
quality to the acidity.

René Barbier Mediterranean Red n.v.   13   £B
Good style here. Better than other René Barbier batches.

Rioja Casa del Marques Sin Crianza 1993   17   £B
One of the best riojas for the money around. Lovely balanced
style with the fruit taking the acidity firmly by the hand. Dry,
damson fruit with a hint of blackcurrant sweetness on the
finish. Has a woodiness achieved, I believe, by the immersion
of oak barrels in the steel vats.

Rioja Cosme Tinto, Bodegas Palacio 1990   16   £C
Balanced, very balanced in fact, with none of the aggressive
woodiness of the old-style rioja. Blackberries and plums
finished drily and deliciously.

Rioja d'Avalos Tempranillo 1993   13   £B

Rioja Tempranillo Berberana 1991   16.5   £C
Biscuity, fruity, gently rich. Superb drinking.

**Señorio de Nava Ribera del Duero Crianza
1987**   14   £C
Fruit dropping out a teeny bit, but superb with a beef stew.

SPANISH WINE – *white*

Augustus Chardonnay, Puig & Roca 1992   18   £F
Delightful toasty aroma of impressive weight – it suggests the
wine will be complex without the wood dominating. And
indeed this is the effect the wine has on my palate. It knocks
Meursaults at three times this price into a cocked hat. An
expensive treat for Christmas. Sit down and enjoy it for the
sheer thrill of it. Sweet oak!

Rioja Cosme Blanco, Bodegas Palacio 1992   15   £C
Deliciously chewy white with the fruit held well by the acid.

Not over-oaked or blowsy.

Rioja d'Avalos Viura 1993   13   £B
White rioja in the frascati mould.

USA WINE – *red*

Crichton Hall Merlot 1991   14.5   £E
Curious merlot. Delicious, but curious.

Saintsbury Carneros Garnet Pinot Noir 1992   13   £E
Gamy, raspberryish, light. Fun.

St Supery Cabernet Sauvignon 1988   14   £E
Agreeable teeth-coating blackcurrant fruit.

USA WINE – *white*

Crichton Hall Chardonnay 1991   10   £E
Think of it as Puligny-Montrachet and the £10 price tag
won't seem a high price at all.

Kah-Nock-Tie Konocti Chardonnay 1992   13   £D
Fun, but I'm not sure it's a £6 wine.

SPARKLING WINE/CHAMPAGNE

Champagne Brossault Brut n.v.   15   £E
Lovely, light bubbly with real class. Wonderful taste-bud awakener.

Champagne Brossault Brut Rosé n.v.   16   £F
Delicious rosé with outspoken flavour, freshness and style.

Green Point 1991 n.v. (Australia)   14   £F
Lemony, yet soothing.

Majestic

As far as professional wine buying goes, the Masonic order has but one member and he is as nifty a picker of ripe bottles as you are liable to find. Mr Tony Mason, trading director of Majestic, pulled off yet another coup this summer (stocks by now surely exhausted) when he somehow contrived to smuggle a pricey, complex Châteauneuf-du-Pape into an under-four-quid bottle of Côteaux de Tricastin, a near-neighbour of the illustrious Catholic breed but a somewhat humbler, to put it mildly, appellation. Certainly the impression created by the Tricastin red was one superior to its official status. It had a wonderfully rich, enticing aroma rather like gravy, and the powerful berried fruit was robust and combined silky softness with earthy dryness. It was called Domaine Vergobbi and I mention it to give you an idea of the kind of retailer we are dealing with here. Mr Mason allots a fair whack of his wine-buying budget to snapping up bargains and these are always to be found in the warehouses. Though this can make life a rewarding delight for a wine writer like myself, who enjoys nothing better than putting fantastic wines under his readers' noses, it is equally galling that by definition these wines enjoy a short shelf-life. Often no sooner have I written them up than they have vanished into the black hole which constitutes Majestic's loyal customers' collective thirst.

To wit: Couly-Dutheil's Chinon les Garous 1990 (black-cherry flavours, dry and slaty, yet with that velvet touch in the middle, richly stitched to the surrounding acids); Château Ste Jeanne 1990, a plummy Corbières also offering cherries along with blackcurrant among its fruit and a serious yet amusing wine; Les Jamelles Mourvèdre 1990, a Vin de Pays d'Oc with superbly rounded fruit and just a suspicion of the dark, chewy earthiness of the mourvèdre grape; Montepulciano d'Abruzzo Barone Cornacchia 1992 (squashy blackcurrants and dry raspberries); Notarpanaro Cosimo Taurino 1983, which blitzes the palate with cough-syrupy fruitiness peppered with a subtle liquorice spiciness; Alentejo Tinto Velho 1987 (figs, cherries, plums and a touch of cassis all parcelled up in lovely chewy tannings); and Château d'Aqueria Lirac 1990 (a digestive-biscuit middle to its rich Rhône fruit, with a faint suggestion of barolo about it). Is there a feeling here that the Masons are a red-wine order?

Odd bottles of these terrific wines, however, may still survive in odd Majestics as testimonies to the acute sensibilities of Mr Mason, and I wish you luck if you go hunting, but there are plenty of other splendid bottles in the listings which follow to make up for their lack.

Perhaps it is more to be marvelled at that Majestic is here at all, still in business, still committing itself to digging up toothsome bargains. All high-street wine retailers have enjoyed a far-from-easy trading existence over the past dozen years, but Majestic has not only battled its way through this, it has also, since it started in business fourteen years ago, enjoyed (or endured) several changes of ownership, a restructuring, a merger, a divorce and a remarriage (not all in that order). Mr Mason's curriculum vitae – Oddbins, Augustus Barnett, Majestic, Wizard, then back to Majestic – is reflected, in part, in these upheavals, but let no one doubt that Majestic is here to stay, prosper, expand and generally remain the least superficial oddball option – Oddbins apart – in wine retailing.

It is easily the most attractive place in which to indulge the British sport of wine browsing, and dreamers are often to be seen gazing wistfully at the exotic, expensive bottles (like the 1983 Vieux Château Certain, £29.99), but actually purchasing

a case of Vin de Pays d'Aude Oliviers (£2.19). And a case of
the stuff is what the licensing laws demand, or a full mixed
case, and while this deters the casual pedestrian needing a
single bottle for supper, it does not put off the car owner,
since all the Majestics I have seen have car lots and cheerful
staff ready to wheel the cases out or deliver locally. There is
an excellent range of champagnes and sparkling wines, red
and white bordeaux (with none of the predictable names,
Montrose and Calon Segur apart), a fair body of burgundies
(red and white), and Loire, Rhône, Alsace, and French
regional (red and white). Germany gets a decent shout,
though almost all the rieslings need more bottle age. Italy is
solidly represented in both colours, so is Spain and so is
Portugal (some excellent mid-price reds here). California is in
with more than a shout (red and white), Australia is good (but
perhaps not as outstanding in depth as one might have
thought likely, given Mr Mason's nose), South Africa is weak
(but will improve, I've a hunch), eastern Europe is OK,
England is derisory, New Zealand is middling fair (weak on
reds), and South America is promising if not exactly overwhelming. There are ports, sherries, an excellent range of
beers and lagers, and also mineral waters and spirits.

Indeed, with regard to the latter category I must confess
that Majestic's Calvados du Pays d'Auge, the only calva
appellation worth considering in truth with its unique insis-
tence on double distillation, is a favourite of mine and is a
particular bedtime digestif chez Gluck. Indeed, I must further
confess that a glass of it is at my elbow as I write and it has
made several journeys to my lips as I have written Majestic's
introduction.

Let no one say I do not get into the spirit of a retailer when I
put pen to paper (or, rather, finger to word-processor).

AUSTRALIAN WINE – *red*

Church Hill Shiraz Cabernet 1991   13 £C

Hollick Estate Coonawarra Red 1991   14 £E
Has appley undertones to the fruit which is bright, breezy and
has a delicious concentrated single note of fruit, which is
faintly wild-raspberry flavoured on the finish.

Penfolds Bin 35 Shiraz Cabernet 1992   15 £D
Ripe, soft fruit with some development ahead of it. Attractive
berry flavours, well-structured and balanced. Very drinkable
now, but a 17–18-pointer in three to four years.

Preece Cabernet Sauvignon 1992, Mitchelton   13 £D

Pyrus 1990, Coonawarra, Lindemans   14 £E
A four-grape blend; the usual bordeaux varieties combine to
produce very rich, softly tannic fruit which will, I feel, develop
further over the next two to three years.

Simon Hacket Cabernet Shiraz 1990   14 £C
Zippy and tasty. Has its quirky touches, but its deliciousness
cannot be denied.

Wyndham Estate Shiraz Bin 555 1991   16 £C
A tarry beauty; rich, dank, exotic, potent, pliant and quite
compelling.

AUSTRALIAN WINE – *white*

Church Hill Chardonnay 1993   13 £C

Hollick Estate Chardonnay 1991, Coonawarra   14   £E
Wood and lemon butter. Too full? Not really – just
enthusiastic.

Penfolds Bin 21 Semillon/Chardonnay 1993   15   £C
Fresh and lively, yet a dollop of pineappley melon keeps
intruding. Delicious, refreshing wine.

Penfolds Koonunga Hill Chardonnay 1992   14   £C
Full, lush fruit plus a ticklish dollop of lemon zest. Delicious,
but getting pricey near a fiver.

Penfolds Semillon/Chardonnay 1993   14   £C
Excellent recipe: fruit, acid, wood, but will integrate and
improve mightily over the next one to two years.

Penfolds South Australia Chardonnay 1992   16   £D
Lovely polished, lush, woody fruit with touches of lemon,
beautifully balanced. Elegant – a real alternative, at a far lower
price, to fine burgundy.

Preece Chardonnay 1993, Mitchelton   13   £D
Good, but neither as quirky nor as exciting as previous
vintages.

Wyndhams Estate Bin 222 Chardonnay 1990   15   £C
Lovely melon, lemon and wood combination. Real classy fruit,
rich and buttery, yet fresh and uncloying. Excellent stuff at an
excellent price.

CHILEAN WINE – *red*

**Montenuevo Oak Aged Cabernet Sauvignon 1991,
Vinicola** 14 £C
Tasty yet not overrich or overreaching itself. Delicious to
enjoy by itself.

ENGLISH WINE – *red*

Denbies Red 1992 5 £D
Dilute cherry and greengage juice of unspeakable dullness.
Might be effectively reduced to make a fruit sauce to pour
over wild duck.

FRENCH WINE – *red*

**Beaume-de-Venise Côtes du Rhône Villages
1990** 14 £C
Delicious soft fruit with that dry, earthy touch of Beaume.

**Bourgogne Passetoutgrains 1992, Mongeard-
Mugneret** 11 £C
Burnt-rubber fruit. Great chilled with spicy dishes.

Château Beausejour 1990, Fronsac 14 £D
Superb now, but superber in three to four years' time. Richly
tannic and developing.

Château d'Aqueria, Lirac 1990   16 £D
Sweet, chewy, digestive-biscuit fruit with liquorice-like hints.
Quite, quite delicious.

Château Meaume 1990, Bordeaux Supérieur   13 £C
This is good, but closed at the moment. Another year?

Château Ste Jeanne 1990, Corbières   16 £C
Gorgeous deep, plummy, black cherry and blackcurrant wine.
Serious yet amusing, dry yet giving, full yet not full of itself.

Chinon, Les Bardons 1992   15 £B
Light, soft, raspberry/slate aroma and fruit – delicious! A
beginner's chinon (it's very easygoing on the slate) but very
attractive. Fantastic bargain!

Chinon les Garous 1990, Couly-Dutheil   16 £D
Black cherries, very dry and slate-like, yet soft and ripely
finished. Lovely wine to drink cool with barbecued food.
Indeed, I would consider the highest mark of a civilized host
that (s)he would serve this chilled with charcoal-cooked lamb!

Coteaux de Tricastin 1990, Domaine Vergobbi   18 £C
Wonderful, rich, enticing aroma rather like a gravy. The
powerful berried fruit is superbly robust and polished,
offering both softness yet dryness in classic proportions. It
tastes like a young Châteauneuf-du-Pape, but is priced like an
ordinary beaujolais.

Coudoulet de Beaucastel 1992, Côtes du Rhône 13 £D

Domaine de Guignal 1988, Cahors   13 £B

**Domaine Fouletière 1991, Coteaux du
Languedoc**   13 £C

**Le St-Cricq Vin de Table Rouge, Germain
Pères et Fils n.v.** 11 £A

Les Jamelles Mourvèdre 1992, Vin de Pays d'Oc 15 £C
Superbly rounded fruit with merely a soupçon of the typical
earthiness of mourvèdre. Excellently put together and will age
superbly over one to three years.

Les Jamelles Syrah 1993, Vin de Pays d'Oc 14 £C
Ripe, soft, easy drinking.

**Mercurey Rouge Les Mauvarennes 1991,
Faiveley** 12 £E

**Monastière de Trignan 1992, Coteaux du
Languedoc** 14 £C
Lovely, rich, dusty fruit.

Règnie La Roche Thulon 1992, Louis Latour 13 £D

St-Estèphe 1990, Raoul Johnston 13 £E

St-Joseph 1990, Caves des Papes, Ogier 12 £D

Vin de Pays de l'Aude 13 £A
Soft and cherryish. The label shows a man with his head in a
bucket; either he can't get enough of this wine or he is
recovering from an excess of it. This wine is said to be *délicieux
jusqu'à la dernière goûte.*

**Vin de Pays de Vaucluse 1993, Mark Robertson
and Local Co-op** 13 £B

FRENCH WINE – *white*

**Baron de Hoen Tokay Pinot Gris Vendanges
Tardives 1990**   12   £F
Delicious, perhaps not as ready to drink as it will be in seven to
eight years, and very expensive.

**Bourgogne Chardonnay, 'Georges Faiveley'
1992**   12   £E

**Bourgogne Chardonnay 'Paulee' 1992,
I. Faiveley**   12   £D

**Cante Cigale Rosé de Saignee 1993, Vin de Pays
de l'Herault**   14   £B
Light, fruity, fresh. Good fun with fish or without food.

Chablis 1993, Vocorer   10   £D

Chardonnay 1993, Vin de Pays d'Oc   15   £B
Superb value for money: fruity, dry, subtle yet characterful.
Good buttery side to it.

Château de Sours Rosé 1993, Bordeaux 14   £D
A rich, substantial rosé with modern cherry and pear fruit
aromas.

Château La Fonrousse Monbazillac 1990 16.5 £D
Beautiful bargain dessert wine with a burnt-caramel and honey
edge.

Château Meaume Rosé 1993   15   £C
A seriously delicious rosé.

Chinon Rosé 1992, Couly-Dutheil   14   £D
Earthy, delicious fruity, and superbly ripe and zesty on the finish.

Cuvée Constantin 1991, Max Ferd Richter
Trocken 13 £C
Very attractive aperitif.

Domaine des Granges 1990, Touraine Chenin 14 £C
Delicious fruit, dry and gently rotund, which finishes with the best of chenin-blanc stylishness, with a subtle slap of honey.

Le St-Cricq Blanc de Blancs 1993 15 £A
Bright, modern, very fresh with pear-drop undertones and apple-skin overtones. Brilliant summer drinking.

Les Jamelles Marsannes 1992, Vin de Pays d'Oc 13 £C
Smells a little as if you should toss it in your eye rather than down the throat; reminds me of Optrex. The fruit is muted and rather nun-like in reserve.

Muscat, Vin de Pays des Collines de la Noure
1993, Hugh Ryman 15 £B
A vivid balancing-act of ripe, sweet melon fruit and raunchy acidity. Terrific with hard fruit and hard cheese, or blue cheese by itself.

Pinot Blanc 1993, Laugel 14 £C
Powdery overtones on the melon/peach/apricot fruit. Finishes clean, but slightly muted. Very good price. Excellent aperitif.

Pouilly-Fumé les Loges 1993, Guy Saget 12 £D

Sancerre les Roches 1993, Vacheron 15 £E
Follows the '92 closely in some respects, except it has more intense gooseberry fruit in the mid-palate. Excellent forceful style of middle balance. Expensive, but very sound.

Sauvignon Blanc Comte d'Ormont 1993, Guy
Saget   14   £B
Musty, grassy aromas lead to musty, grassy fruit of huge
appeal to fresh-shellfish eaters.

Tokay Pinot Gris 1992, Ribeauville   15   £D
Superb. Streaks of apricot fruit, chewy yet not soft or flabby,
mingle with the firm acids to make a superb aperitif.

GERMAN WINE – –*white*

Piesporter Goldtröpfchen Riesling Auslese 1990,
Reichsgraf von Kesselstatt   15   £E
Marvellous kerosene echoes in the fruit, gentle acidity not
overwhelming it. An aperitif of finesse and sophistication.

Trittenheimer Altarchen Riesling Kabinett
1990   15   £E
Seductive lime-sherbet, zesty aroma, striking lemon-sherbety
acids and fruit. You could probably mix it with gin. Delicious
drink to have in one's hand while listening to a close friend's
tale of woe.

ITALIAN WINE – *red*

Montepulciano d'Abruzzo 1992, Barone
Cornacchia   16   £C
Deft, squashy blackcurrant and raspberries (as is the
d'Abruzzo style), but unusual dryness. Superb value.

Notarpanaro 1983, Cosimo Taurino 16 £C
Deep, cough-syrup undertones to the brisk fruit (suspiciously brisk, considering it's sitting its 11-plus) – slight spiciness and liquorice quality. Lovely stuff.

**Recioto della Valpolicella Halves 1988,
Tedeschi** 15 £D
Prunes and figs in sweet harmony. A wine to drink with black grapes.

San Crispino Sangiovese di Romagna 1990 14 £D
Superb chewy fruit.

**Santara Red 1993, Conca de Barbera, Hugh
Ryman** 14 £B
Good dry fruit, nicely shrouded in tannins, yet soft and tongue tickling. Very good value.

ITALIAN WINE – *white*

La Prendina Bianco 1993, Vino da Tavola 13 £D
Delicious. Expensive.

Vin Santo Brolio 1985, Ricasoli 14 £D
An interesting example of a wine I usually detest. This has muted marmalade fruit and would be great with treacle tart or sticky-toffee pudding.

NEW ZEALAND WINE – *red*

Coopers Creek Cabernet Merlot 1991, Huapai   13   £E

Delegat's Proprietor's Reserve Cabernet Sauvignon
1991   14   £E

NEW ZEALAND WINE – *white*

Coopers Creek Chardonnay 1993, Gisborne   16   £D
Woody, oily, polished and balanced. A lovely chardonnay with
lots of flavour and style.

Coopers Creek Sauvignon 1993, Gisborne   15   £C
Delicious fruit with a lovely pineapple/lemon lift to the finish.
Not herbaceously strident in the least.

Coopers Creek Sauvignon 1993, Marlborough   14   £D
Ripe touches to the fruit coolly dominating the acidity. Pleasant aperitif.

Goldwater Chardonnay 1992, Marlborough   12   £E

Oyster Bay Chardonnay 1993, Marlborough   15   £E
Balanced beauty. Tasteful fruit playing fast and loose with the
acidity in fine style.

Oyster Bay Sauvignon 1993, Marlborough   14   £D
Flavourful and concentrated.

PORTUGUESE WINE – *red*

Bairrada Sanafeira 1980   14   £B
Surprising price for a 14-year-old wine. Solid, fruity, only a
little dry at the edges and very good with rich foods.

SOUTH AFRICAN WINE – *red*

Backsberg Klein Babylonstoren 1990, Paarl   13   £D

Backsberg Shiraz 1990   14   £D
Beaten leather, dried plums and a faint liquorice tingle.

SOUTH AFRICAN WINE – *white*

Backsberg Chardonnay 1991, Paarl   15   £D
Quiet, restrained, mature. Give it a pipe and a pair of slippers
and it'll entertain you for hours. Has the delicacy of good
manners and breeding.

SPANISH WINE – *red*

Alentejo Tinto Velho 1987, J. M. da Fonseca   16   £C
Figs and cherries, plums and cassis – all wrapped in tannins of
marvellous firm chewability. Lovely rich-food wine (cheeses
especially).

Berberana Reserva Rioja 1986   14 £C
Young and gamy, surprising spring in its step for an eight-year-old.

Viña Real Gran Reserva Rioja 1982   13 £F
Delicious. Expensive.

Viñedos d'Avalos Rioja 1987   15 £C
Creamy, soft, not overblown. Great red just to savour by itself.

SPANISH WINE – *white*

Viñedos d'Avalos Rioja 1987   15 £C
Woody aromas, somewhat rudely planed, but the fruit has vigour and attack and with creamy fish dishes or grilled chicken would be superb. Also good with barbecues.

USA WINE – *white*

Calera Chardonnay, Central Coast 1990   15 £F
Decidedly a one-off and quite delicious. Has a solid-wood note to it and this chimes well with the fullish fruit, but there's a bizarre and intriguing elegance to the whole thing which tickles the palate and fires the imagination at one and the same time.

Electra Orange Muscat 1991, Andrew Quady   15 £C
Enjoy this high-voltage sweet wine with its exotic fruit content (lime and mango juice) as an aperitif.

Elysium Black Muscat 1993, Andrew Quady 15 £D
Cassis-like. Try it with blackcurrant fool.

Essensia Orange Muscat Halves 1992,
Andrew Quady 14 £D
Extraordinary stuff. Superbly rich and sweet, and great with
strawberry tart.

SPARKLING WINE/CHAMPAGNE

Ayala Champagne n.v. 13 £F
Invariably delicious, this *marque*. Classic champagne.

Chantelore Brut Blanc de Blancs n.v. (France) 14 £C
Confectionery fruit fizz up front, then pleasant, fresh acid
sidles in. An excellent summer-garden aperitif – as long as
you're not expecting a Bollinger clone.

Chantelore Rosé n.v. (France) 14 £C
Touch of ice-cream strawberry fruit in the middle. Good for
gardens, hot days, and letting it all hang out.

De Telmont Grande Reserve Champagne n.v. 12 £F
Raspberry-meringue fruit. Never tasted a champagne like it
before.

Lancelot de Hoen Crémant d'Alsace n.v. 14 £E
Butter-biscuit fruit. Rather attractive in a raffish sort of way.

Oeil de Perdrix NV, Leonce d'Albe n.v. 15 £F
Excellent value and much more concentrated and fine than
many grand *marques*. Creamy, nutty undertones.

**Seppelt Chardonnay Blanc de Blancs Brut 1990
(Australia)**   13   £E
Solid, dependable, gently citric bubbly.

Seppelt Great Western Brut n.v. (Australia)   16   £C
Superb bargain. A finer fizzer on sale for under a fiver it's
difficult to name. Lemony, zingy, zesty. Great style.

Seppelt Great Western Rosé n.v.   15   £D

Shadow Creek 1986 (USA)   11   £E

Taittinger n.v.   11   £G

Taltarni Brut Tache n.v. (Australia)   13   £E

Oddbins

Everyone in high-street wine retailing would like to be like Oddbins, but only Oddbins can be. It invokes envy. It induces jealousy. It inspires admiration. It provokes imitation.

It also produces angry puzzlement. 'How do they stay in business?' the director of wine buying of a bigger competitor once rhetorically asked me some three or four years ago. I waited for a moment for the froth around his mouth to subside. 'Seagrams puts its hands in its pocket, that's how,' he proceded to tell me. I later discovered that this person regularly checked the figures of all wine businesses obliged to register their accounts at Companies House, 55 City Road, London EC1, but which are open to inspection upon paying a small fee to the Department of Trade and Industry. He failed, however, to provide further detailed evidence to support this claim. In any case, it could hardly be a fact which would surprise me. What else would Seagrams do but support their baby?

Seagrams bought Oddbins some years ago initially, I would guess, as a distribution vehicle for its own wine brands because its ambitions to develop and market these products were continually frustrated by vested interests behind the brands stocked by high-street retailers. Seagrams is a remarkable company. It values individuality – perhaps because it has built much of its business by developing and buying individual brands (Chivas Regal, for example) to which consumers feel an individual loyalty. The company has a huge reservoir of patience allied to an entrepreneurial flair peculiar in a multinational organization so vast, so profitable, so politically well connected, and so widespread (it has more whiskies, bourbons, tequilas, vodkas, gins and whathaveyou than the average cocktail lounge has in its annual turnover of bar flies). And here lies the root of other retailers' irritation at Oddbins' success.

Other retailers cannot stand the fact that the kid on the block with the richest dad gets to do as he likes. Oddbins' competitors envy Oddbins for the freedom it has enjoyed when they themselves have, until lately, been curtailed by straight thinking and a committee mentality which is anti-thetical to innovation and fresh ideas. Nothing shocks (at first) a large retail company so much as when a significant com-petitor does something outrageous (like responding to market trends and changes in customers' habits). The shock develops into envy when the outrage is seen to attract business.

It wasn't fair when Oddbins came along and broke all the rules. Buying wines from areas the other blokes had hardly heard of (Australia! It's all desert, isn't it?). Refusing to visit South Africa on political grounds or to consider cheap bottles from eastern Europe because the wines weren't good enough. Since when did politics and a lousy product stop an honest man making an honest bob or two? And have you seen the sort of staff they employ? They may know a thing or two about wine, *but they wear jeans and some of them even have beards!* And as for the wine list! Gerald Scarfe at his most horrifically inspired and ingenious! And have you been inside one of the shops? I've seen a smarter wood shed after it's been done over by a gang of graffiti artists. Pity the poor retailers who gnashed their teeth and watched their customers desert them. Oddbins was so far ahead of the other retailers it was embarrassing. Seagrams, true to its unusual corporate mentality, didn't stick an oar in when it wasn't needed and they didn't pull the plug when things got tight. Possibly, it was just as bemused at Oddbins' success as its competitors were.

And so Oddbins has grown into the André Agassi of wine retailers. (Except that André would need to win Wimbledon every year to make that analogy fit properly.) It now has 186 branches, a fledgeling new development in fine-wine shops, and the most distinctive profile of any wine business in any high street.

It also has some terrific buyers, a tireless PR department, some sparkling advertising, a superbly readable wine list, a range of wines with some incomparable strengths, and over and above all this is the fact that a generation of wine drinkers – important opinion-forming wine drinkers – have, throughout the 1980s and throughout the recession, and increasingly now the worst of the recession is over, stayed loyal. In spite of Thresher launching Wine Rack, Victoria Wine introducing its Wine Cellars shops, Cellar 5 announcing Berkeley Wines, and Wizard and Majestic becoming a sum greater than the parts, Oddbins is ahead of them all in the fierceness of its focus and the quality of its innovation. I do not say its wines are better than other wine retailers', or that it even offers so tasty or so consistent a bunch of bargains, but the face which it turns to the world is the most acceptable face in high-street wine retailing in Britain. Seagrams has let the company grow at its own pace (it absorbed Gough Brothers with barely an audible hiccup), expanded rather than exploded (only fifty-five branches added in the past six years), and stayed true to its roots (which have always bin odd).

In a world where the supermarkets have become the dominant wine retailers in this country, Oddbins is a healthy child of genius born out of commercial frivolity, and sustained by a wise and indulgent foster parent. Never did a retailer have such wonderful advantages and long may it continue to enjoy them.

The wines? I almost forgot the wines. Well, forget eastern

Europe and South Africa. Marvel at Australia and Chile (incomparable ranges both). Goggle at New Zealand. Ignore the sillier wines from California in an otherwise superb collection. Lose yourself in Spain and Italy. France isn't bad either – Bordeaux is particularly well chosen and sound value, the Rhône is terrific, and Alsace, the Loire and Vin de Pays are exceptional to good. Germany is wonderful (so wonderful that when I took part in a German-wine-producer-inspired lunch matching German wines to food and the majority of the German wines in attendance turned out to be naff, it was to the local Oddbins branch we turned for great bottles – notably Müller–Catoir). Champagnes are sparkling, so is a magnificent selection of bubblies (superb Prosecco).

You can treat your local Oddbins as you would treat your nearest branch of Waterstones: a wonderful place to browse and to strike up a casual conversation with a stranger whom you re-encounter at the cash till, clutching the same bottle (book). To end up, perhaps, gazing across the same menu in the same restaurant. Can you see this happening at Waitrose? Can you see it happening at Victoria Wine? With the best will in the world I cannot (yet).

I'll tell you something else. No high-street wine buyer can more quickly suss a corked wine, however subtle its effect, than Oddbins' Steve Daniel. And no high-street wine buyer has a tighter focus on exactly the kind of fruit, both red and white, his customers enjoy in their wines. It's an uncommon knack.

ARGENTINIAN WINE – *red*

Trapiche Pinot Noir 1992 13 £C
Delightful sweet fruit.

AUSTRALIAN WINE – *red*

Angoves Nanya Estate Grenache/Pinot Noir n.v.   8   £B
This has got to be the naffest Aussie red I have tasted for
some years. Sticking grenache with pinot noir is like asking
Jane Torvill to ice-dance with Paul Gascoigne.

Baileys Shiraz 1992   15   £D
This leathery, furry-fruited wine may well be descended from
the one which sozzled Ned Kelly, for it was in the Victorian
hamlet of Glenrowan, where Baileys built their winery in
1870, that the law finally caught the drunken bandit. Baileys
Shiraz grabs the drinker by the throat every bit as effectively,
though somewhat more affectionately, as the noose from
which the rogue finally swung. Linctus-like texture offering
layered fruits, blackcurrants to plums, with touches of tobacco
and coffee. Superb.

Coldstream Hills Pinot Noir 1992   12   £E

Geoff Merrill Mount Hurtle Grenache/Shiraz
1992   14   £C

Glenloth Shiraz/Cabernet Sauvignon n.v.   14   £B
Good value here.

Killawarra Cabernet Sauvignon/Shiraz 1992   15   £C
Soft fruit you could pour like squash. Good value.

Killawarra Shiraz/Cabernet 1992   11   £C

Leasingham Clare Shiraz 1992   14   £D

Leeuwin Estate Redgum Ridge Cabernet
Sauvignon 1990   15   £E
Delicious fruit, structure and style.

Lindemans Bin 45 Cabernet Sauvignon 1992   14   £C
Attractive berry flavours and residual richness.

Lindemans Pyrus 1988   15   £E
Lovely subtle eucalyptus touches to the fruit – incredibly unctuous fruit, velvet, soft and yielding.

Lindemans St George Vineyard Cabernet Sauvignon 1989   16   £E
Elegant, soft and smooth – an immediate fruitiness of quiet yet decidedly cassis-like concentration.

McWilliams Mount Pleasant Cabernet Sauvignon 1992   15   £C
Ripe, very soft and yummy.

McWilliams Mount Pleasant Cabernet/Merlot 1992   14   £C
Soft echoes of mint, blackberries/currants. Delicious.

Mount Hurtle Grenache Shiraz 1992   13   £C

Penfolds Bin 2 Shiraz/Mourvèdre 1992   15   £C
Plum and black cherries, muted spice. Delicious! Will develop and get even better.

Penfolds Bin 35 Shiraz Cabernet 1992   15   £C
Ripe, soft fruit with some development ahead of it. Attractive berry flavours, well-structured and balanced. Very drinkable now but a 17–18-pointer in three to four years.

Penfolds Bin 407 Cabernet Sauvignon 1990   16   £E
Superb specimen. Soft fruit with blackcurrant flavour in solid, impressive form.

Penfolds Coonawarra Cabernet Sauvignon 1990   17   £E
The colour of crushed blackberries, subtle eucalyptus/leather

aroma, sheer-satiny acids and velvet-textured fruit touches –
lovely tannicky finish.

Peter Lehmann Shiraz 1991   15   £C
Ripe flavours, well-knitted structure, good firm length.

Ralph's Shiraz 1990   12   £E
A wonderful rich brew for £3.99, but not £9.99.

Saltram Cabernet Sauvignon 1993   14   £C

Saltram Shiraz 1993   14   £C

Tulloch Hunter Valley Shiraz/Cabernet 1988   12   £C

Tulloch Shiraz 1988   14   £C
Delicious, honey-soft shiraz.

**Yalumba Menzies Coonawarra Cabernet Sauvignon
1990**   14   £D
Polished, smooth, gently eucalyptic fruit of quiet finesse. Best
with simple roast meats rather than highly flavoured dishes.

AUSTRALIAN WINES – *white*

Aussie Rules Sauvignon/Semillon 1992   12   £D
Not hugely Aussie in style (so why the name?), as it's bordeaux
copy, but it isn't much of a French wine either.

Bridgewater Mill Chardonnay 1992   12   £D

Bridgewater Mill Sauvignon Blanc 1993   11   £D

Château Reynella Stony Hill Chardonnay 1990   15   £D
Gorgeous, oily, woody fruit with a lush, sweet fruit note on the
finish. Lovely wine at a good price for the excellence of the style.

Cockatoo Ridge Chardonnay 1993　　　　14　£C
Delicious. Full of fruit and good humour.

Coldstream Hills Reserve Chardonnay 1992　　13　£F
A beautiful wine. Not a beautiful price.

Cullen Chardonnay 1992　　　　　　　14　£E
Yes, it's delicious, elegant, sophisticated and I'm in love with
the two women who make it. OK?

Cullen Sauvignon Blanc 1992　　　　　15　£E
A gorgeous s.b. of great individuality and lemonic oomph.
Expensive, but delicious.

De Bortoli Yarra Glen Chardonnay 1991　　14　£D

Glenloth Dry White 1993　　　　　　　14　£B
Lots of ripe fruit plus a touch of gooseberry and pineapple on
the finish. Excellent value.

Glenloth Late Harvest Muscat 1993　　　14　£B
Cheap thrills with hard fruit and cheese for company.

Hardy's R.R. 1993　　　　　　　　　11　£C

**Hindmarsh Hills Barossa Valley Chenin Blanc
1993**　　　　　　　　　　　　　13　£B
Some attractive fruit.

Krondorf Show Reserve Chardonnay 1992　　15　£E
A lovely chewy chardonnay of huge style and class. Classic
book wine.

Leeuwin Estate Chardonnay 1988　　　　12　£G

Lenswood Chardonnay 1992　　　　　10　£E

Lindemans Bin 65 Chardonnay 1993　　　16　£C
Deep-bruised fruit – lovely and ripe. Superb effect on the tongue.

Lindemans Cawarra Colombard 1993   14 £C
Very attractive, rounded fruit which finishes dry.

Lindemans Cawarra, Colombard Chardonnay
1993   14 £C
Ripe fruit character with pineapple fruit-drop acidity.
Delicious.

Mitchelton Goulburn Riesling 1993   11 £C

Mitchelton Reserve Chardonnay 1990   16 £D
Very amusing fogey. Wears a waistcoat and carpet slippers
and tells very fruity jokes.

Mount Hurtle Chardonnay 1992   14 £C
Richness, flavour, style – a great grilled-chicken wine or with
spicy mussels.

Mount Langi Ghiran Riesling 1993   11 £D

Oxford Landing Sauvignon Blanc 1993   14 £C
An excellent bottle of rather oily sauvignon blanc which is not
especially s.b. in feel but who cares? It's jolly tasty.

Penfolds Bin 21 Semillon/Chardonnay 1993   15 £C
Fresh and lively, yet a dollop of pineappley melon keeps
intruding. Delicious, refreshing wine.

Penfolds Bin 202 South Australian Riesling
1993   14 £C
Superb, rich aperitif. Delicious.

Penfolds Koonunga Hill Chardonnay 1992   14 £C
Full, lush fruit plus a ticklish dollop of lemon zest. Delicious,
but getting pricey near a fiver.

Penfolds Semillon/Chardonnay 1993   14 £C
Excellent recipe: fruit, acid, wood but will integrate and

improve mightily over the next one to two years.

Penfolds South Australia Chardonnay 1992   16   £D
Lovely, polished, lush, woody fruit with touches of lemon, beautifully balanced. Elegant – a real alternative, at a far lower price, to fine burgundy.

Peter Lehmann Vine Vale Riesling 1993   11   £C

Pikes Clare Valley Chardonnay 1992   13   £E
Quiet, firmly fruity chardonnay of only moderate charms. Well made, but rather expensive.

Riddoch Katnook Estate Sauvignon Blanc 1992   14   £D
Fresh, grassy nose tinged with lime. Soft, sour gooseberry fruit. Nutty edge to the finish. Interesting seafood wine. Excellent with fresh oysters.

Salisbury Chardonnay 1992   15   £C
There's a lot going on – except with the price. You like fruit? Here it is.

Saltram Chardonnay 1993   14   £C
With a spicy fish gumbo, this is your wine.

Saltram Mamre Brook Chardonnay 1993   15   £D
A completely preoccupied bastard! How can a wine so young be so cocksure? Lovely ripe fruit and undercutting lemony acids.

Saltram Riesling 1993   12   £C

Shaw and Smith Reserve Chardonnay 1992   13   £E

Shaw and Smith Sauvignon Blanc 1993   14   £E
A lot of money, but a lot of style – very attractive s.b.

Valley Estates Rhine Riesling 1993   13   £B
Nice price for a nice mouthful of rich fruit polished up with

some suggestion of freshness on the finish. Not a huge varietal
success, but a bargain aperitif.

Wynn's Riesling 1993   12   £C

CHILEAN WINE – *red*

Caliterra Cabernet Sauvignon 1991   14   £C
Very good value.

Caliterra Cabernet Sauvignon Reserve 1990   15   £C
Rich bouquet of leather and lovely, savoury, rich, gravy-like
fruit. This wine is outstandingly structured. Soft, velvety, very
classy stuff; dry, with exciting claret style and high-class fruit
– but is it slightly too old?

**Casablanca Miraflores Estate Cabernet Sauvignon
1990**   13   £C

Cono Sur Cabernet Sauvignon 1992   12   £D

Cono Sur Pinot Noir Chimbarango 1993   12   £C

Cono Sur Pinot Noir Reserve 1993   13   £D

**Cono Sur Rauli Cabernet Sauvignon/Merlot
1993**   13   £B

**San Fernando Valley Cabernet Sauvignon,
Miraflores Estate 1990**   14   £C
A delicious, soft, approachable wine.

CHILEAN WINE – *white*

Caliterra Chardonnay 1992   14 £C
Lovely melon/lemon style. Again, not huge. A touch expensive, but it has got style.

Caliterra Chardonnay 1993   15 £C
Delicious, slightly woody fruit which is very controlled and fine.

Caliterra Chardonnay Reserve 1992   16 £D
Too expensive for the fruit style which is better represented elsewhere for less money, particularly the Caliterra 1993 Chardonnay.

Caliterra Sauvignon Blanc 1993   16 £C
Elegant, slightly lemon fruit, classy, demure, not tough. Lovely clear aperitif wine. Excellent structure.

Casablanca Chardonnay 1993   14 £C

Casablanca Chardonnay Lontue Valley 1993   13 £C
A completely made wine, but for a penny change out of a fiver I demand more thrills.

Casablanca Sauvignon Blanc 1993   14 £C
Very ripe sauvignon.

Casablanca 'Valley' Gewürztraminer 1993   12 £D

Casablanca 'Valley' Chardonnay, Santa Isabel Estate 1993   13 £D
Some elegance here.

Santa Carolina Chardonnay 1993   16.5 £C
Beautiful wine: demure yet striking, fruity yet discreet, fresh but not tarty.

Santa Carolina Chardonnay, Los Toros Vineyard
1993   15   £C
Soft wood encroaches upon the nose, delicious fruit with a
delightful dry yet almost cherry-fruit edge to it touches the
palate, and a lingering finish stays in the throat.

Santa Carolina Chardonnay Special Reserve,
Santa Rosa Vineyard 1993   13   £D
I would stuff this bottle away for a couple of years – it will
blossom beautifully.

Santa Carolina Reserve Chardonnay 1993   15   £D
Classy, attractive, very firm and fruity, with gentle almond
undertones.

Santa Carolina Sauvignon Blanc 1993   16   £C
Brilliant construction: lemon, melon, peach, pineapple – all
smoothed out and integrated. A classy bargain.

Santa Carolina Sauvignon Blanc, Santa Rosa
Vineyard 1993   15   £C
A lovely, richly finished, slightly fat sauvignon blanc of nicely
turned fruit, good acid balance and overall classiness of structure. Excellent with fish; superb, in fact.

FRENCH WINE – *red*

Château de France, Pessac-Léognan 1989   15   £E
Gamey aroma, gorgeous cherry finish.

Château de Jau, Côtes de Roussillon Villages
1991   14   £C
Excellent structure and dry fruit.

Château de l'Hôpital, Graves 1991   14   £E
Classy, smooth, arrogant.

**Château Haut-Bertinerie Blanc, Premier Côtes
de Blaye 1992**   15   £D
Fresh, light, very flouncy-skirted and fun.

Château Lilian Ladouys, St-Estèphe 1990   15   £E
Lovely blackcurrant fruit. Very distinguished in feel.

Château Paul Blanc 1992, Costière de Nîmes   13   £C

**Château Thieuley, Francis Courselle, Bordeaux
1992**   11   £E

Côtes du Rhône Guigal 1990   13   £C
Not as rich or spicy as usual, but still highly drinkable. But is
Guigal slipping?

**Croix Belle Rouge, Vin de Pays des Côtes de
Thongue 1993**   13   £C
Nice touch of burnt fruit.

Crozes-Hermitage, Les Pierelle 1991, Belle   13   £D

**Domaine Rombeau Cuvée Élise 1991, Côtes du
Roussillon**   14   £C

**Domaine Villerambert Minervois, Cuvée Opéra
1992**   13   £C

Gevrey-Chambertin, Rossignol-Trapet 1991   12   £E

Le Radical Côtes du Ventoux, Le Rouret   12   £B

Le Radical Grenache 1993   14   £B
Very pleasant cherry fruit of a gently hairy mien.

Le Second de Reynon 1992   14 £C
Some seriously attractive dry tannins here. Age for three to
four years.

Michel Lynch Bordeaux Rouge 1990   12 £E
An overrated wine of some charm in the middle, but little
effective structure either side. Very expensive for the paucity
of style on offer.

FRENCH WINE – *white*

Alsace Gewürztraminer, Schoffit 1992   13 £E
A delicious wine of powdery fruit and muskiness.

Alsace Pinot Blanc, Schoffit 1992   12 £D

Chardonnay, Vin de Pays d'Oc 1993, A. Hardy 15 £C
Lashings of bright fruit, melony and full, with an undercutting
whiplash of nuts and pineapple on the finish.

Château Roquefort, 1992   16 £D
Nothing cheesy about this stylishly bright wine; it takes on the
best New Zealand sauvignon blancs and goes the distance
with a ripe aroma of paw-paw and melon and, odd though it
sounds, a faint echo of yoghurt, but this is deliciously
balanced by the gentle zippiness of lemon peel underpinning
the whole construction. Superb with smoked fish of any kind.

**Domaines St-Hilaire Chardonnay, Vin de Pays
d'Oc 1993**   15 £C
Very good fruit here, stylish and sure of itself. But also
balanced and of great interest to grilled-chicken chewers.

La Révolution 1992   12 £D

Le Second de Clos Floridène Blanc 1992   16   £D
Very classy wine: lush wood/fruit integration, calm acidity,
overall purpose and style. Very attractive. Wonderful with
seafood.

Mâcon Davayé, Domaine des Deux Roches
1993   14   £D
An outstanding fruity Mâcon. It has more flavour than a
whole case of the usual Mâcon blancs.

Meursault, Michelot-Buisson 1992   13   £F
Some warmth to the fruit but hopelessly outclassed by Cali-
fornian chardonnays at the price.

Pinot Blanc, Schoffit 1992   14   £D
A delicious pinot blanc with sufficient (though subtle) apricot-
flavoured fruit to be a pinot grigio.

Pouilly-Fuissé Cuvée Vieilles Vignes 1992   13   £F

Puligny-Montrachet Premier Cru J. M. Boillot
1992   13   £H
A very fine piece of fruit. Surely a very low-yielding vineyard,
but too young to drink now, for its rich, perfectly poised fruit
will improve hugely over time: 13 points now; 18 from 1998
on.

Riesling, Schoffit 1992   12   £E

St-Aubin, Premier Cru Clos de la Chatemique
1992   12   £F

St-Véran 1992   13   £E

St-Véran, Close Les Chailloux, Domaine des Deux
Roches 1992   14   £D
Lots of fruit and flavour! What's going on in Burgundy? Or is

it just Stephen Daniel, Oddbins' wine buyer, being very, very shrewd?

Sauvignon Blanc, Vin de Pays d'Oc 1993   14   £C
Lots of fruit for a sauvignon blanc, ripe but with enough compensating acids to let you know this is a sauvignon.

Terret Blanc, Vin de Pays d'Oc 1993   14   £B
Modern pear-drop aromas and fruit, very perky and fresh too.

GERMAN WINE – *white*

**Haardter Herzog Riesling Spätlese Trocken
Müller-Catoir, Rheinpfalz 1992**   12   £E

**Haardter Mandelring Scheurebe Spätlese
Müller-Catoir, Rheinpfalz 1992**   14   £E
Lovely, flowery stuff.

**Mussbacher Eselshaut Riesling Auslese
Müller-Catoir, Rheinpfalz 1992**   16   £G
Magnificent.

**Neustadter Mönchgarten Weisserburgunder Kabinett
Trocken Müller-Catoir, Rheinpfalz 1992**   11   £E

ITALIAN WINE – *red*

Barbera Piemonte, S. Orsola n.v.   13   £B
Soft and pretty.

Primitivo del Salento 1993, Le Trulle   13   £C

Puglian Red, The Country Collection 1993   14   £B
Delicious, cherry-ripe value for money.

Ronco delle Torre Cabernet Sauvignon 1990   13   £D

ITALIAN WINE – *white*

Chardonnay del Salento 1993, Kym Milne   15   £C
Beautiful structure, lovely fruit, good acidity. Terrific value.

Riva White 1993   16   £B
Such ripe fruit for the money! Fantastic ripe fruit! Fantastic!
Ripe! Gorgeous! Unctuous!

MOLDOVAN WINE – *white*

Chardonnay Hinesti 1992   11   £B
Rather sweet for a chardonnay and not overly balanced.

Chardonnay St-Hilaire 1992   15   £C
An excellent, oily, rounded fruity white of great style and
verve. An *interesting* chardonnay.

Rkatsiteli Hincesti 1992   12   £B
Fascinating little aperitif.

NEW ZEALAND WINE – *white*

Brothers Semillon/Sauvignon 1992   14   £D
Lushly touched fruit from the semillon matched by vivid
perkiness of the sauvignon.

Giesen Sauvignon Blanc 1993   13   £D

Montana Sauvignon Blanc 1993   13   £C

PORTUGUESE WINE – *red*

Borba 1992   14   £B

Warre LBV Port 1981   15   £F
Rich, prune-like port of admirably classic structure and feel.
Delicious.

PORTUGUESE WINE – *white*

Bairrada, Quinta do Ribeiruho 1990   14   £C

SOUTH AFRICAN WINE – *white*

Danie de Wet Chardonnay 1993   13   £C
This was not drinking hugely impressively – even the citric style
was muted. I miss the touch of oak which Danie does so well, too.

SPANISH WINE – *red*

Agramont Cabernet/Tempranillo 1990,
Navarra   15 £C
Lovely, biscuity tannins shrouding the blackcurrant fruit
beautifully.

Campillo 1988, Rioja   15 £D
Ripe, austere fruit.

Garnacha 1993, Navarra   16 £C
Superb fruit. Exceptionally rich and ripe, without being
overblown.

Las Torres 1992   11 £D
I can't recommend drinking this wine until late 1995 or '96. It
fails to reach the peaks of taste and complexity Miguel Torres
always aims for and this fine wine needs time to develop. It is
soft and drinkable now, but not half as rich and flavourful as,
for example, Portuguese reds from the Alentejo or Ribolejo at
half the price.

Palacio de la Vega 1991   14 £C
Rich, ripe wine of plum fruit, with an edge of Marmite. Very
attractive food wine.

Palacio de la Vega Cabernet Sauvignon 1991,
Navarra   15 £D
Superbly bright, supporting tannins in a dry, fruity wine of
some class.

Palacio de la Vega Cabernet/Tempranillo 1991,
Navarra   15 £C
Terrifically elegant fruit.

Puelles 1992 Rioja   16   £C
Deeply attractive, very complete and well finished, and by
Jesus it's great. By Jesus Puelles, that is, the wine-maker. A
touch luscious. Very untypical but very delicious.

Rioja Cosme Tinto, Bodegas Palacio 1990   16   £C
Balanced. Very balanced in fact, with none of the aggressive
woodiness of the old-style rioja. Blackberries and plums
finished drily and deliciously.

Solana Red 1993, Navarra   16   £C
Vivid fruit, quite startlingly black cherry and plum. And soft?
You could lay your head on it.

Torres Gran Coronas 1988   15   £E
Silken, soft, rich, but very demure at the same time, this wine
is a curiously un-Torres-like ensemble: it seems more like
some third-growth bordeaux from a once-great château which
has eccentrically produced a lovely wine.

Valedepomares 1992, Rioja   14   £B
Soft, plummy, lovely little sweet-fruit finish, then dryness.

Vega de Moriz 1993, Valdepeñas   15   £B
Lots of ripe fruit flavours, some tannins and acid – an excellently structured, seriously good wine for the money.

Vega de Rio, Rioja 1992   14   £B
This is a cherry and strawberry-fruited plonk of unequivocal
charm: simple, direct, delicious. A bottle to open for the sheer
delight of quaffing £2.99 wine; an excellent bottle, indeed, to
accompany *Coronation Street*, especially when Ken Barlow is
attempting to master the complexities of red wine and red-
headed women at one and the same time.

SPANISH WINE – *white*

Agramont Viura 1993, Navarra   14   £C
Gentle little aperitif.

José Bezares, Rioja Blanco 1988   14   £C
Good, oily fruit, full yet not overripe or overrich.

Rioja Cosme Blanco, Bodegas Palacio 1992   15   £C
Delightful chewy white, with the fruit held well by the acid. Not
over-oaked or blowsy.

Sauvignon Blanc 1993, Lurton, Rueda   15   £C
Gorgeous, aromatic, floral aperitif. Lovely ripe fruit, well-
matched by the citric fruited acidity. Deliciously unstoppable
(i.e., you can't leave the bottle half-empty to finish tomorrow).

Solana, Ribero 1993   15   £C
Lovely combo of melon fruit and gentle lemon/pineapple
acidity.

USA WINE – *red*

Benziger Cabernet Sauvignon 1991   13   £D
Good, soft, soggy fruit.

Fetzer Petite Syrah, Eagle Point Vineyard 1991   16   £D
A feisty pudding of a wine, with lots of baked and candied-fruit
flavours. Rich, soupy, tannic and very dry. Hairy and handsome.

Franciscan Cabernet Sauvignon 1991   13   £D

Franciscan Monterey Pinot Noir 1991   12   £D

USA WINE – *white*

Benziger Chardonnay 1991   15   £D
Loadsa fruit.

Bloody Good White 1993   15   £D
As by name, so by nature. Complex, rich, full, satisfying. Has
gentle muscat, 'overripe' grape and lush acidity.

Fetzer Zinfadel 1990   14   £C
Soft, berried fruit, touch of sweet spice.

Franciscan Chardonnay 1992   15   £D
A ripe, toasty, butter-rich wine of compelling gluggability.

Franciscan Oakville Estate Cuvée Sauvage
1991   15   £E
Lemony, woody, classy; the product of tightly focused wine-
making aiming at fruit-wood integration at the highest level.

Kiona Late Harvest Riesling 1990   13   £D
Quirky individual sweetie.

Montevina Fumé Blanc, Napa 1991   13   £C
Keen grass-cuttings nose – unusual sweetly touched fruit.
Rather a curious animal altogether, since it isn't an aperitif
and I'm jiggered if I can figure out what food it goes with.

Ridge Santa Cruz Chardonnay 1990   13   £G

Wild Horse Chardonnay 1992   15   £E
Custardy and full of flavour – very charismatic.

SPARKLING WINE/CHAMPAGNE

Billecart-Salmon n.v.   16   £G
Elegance, style, aplomb.

Cuvée Napa Rosé n.v.   14   £E
Great stuff.

Pierre Gimonnet Champagne 1989   15   £G
Vivid structure. Lay down and it'll improve for two to three years.

Roger Blanc de Blanc Champagne n.v.   13   £F

Seaview Brut n.v.   15   £D
Where available for under £5, one of the best sparklers on the market: stylish, refined, and quite delicious.

**Seaview Pinot Noir/Chardonnay 1990
(Australian)**   15   £E
Mature, fruity, classy. Great value.

Segura Viudas n.v.   13   £D

Seppelt Great Western Brut n.v. (Australia)   16   £C
Superb bargain. A finer fizzer on sale for under a fiver it's difficult to name. Lemony, zingy, zesty. Great style.

Seppelt Great Western Rosé n.v.   15   £D

Seppelt Pinot Rosé Cuvée Brut Sparkling n.v.   15   £D
Delicious. Real fruit here, justifying the colour.

Seppelt Premier Cuvée Brut   15   £D
Lovely fizz, light and handsome.

**Seppelt Salinger Sparkling Wine n.v.
(Australia)**   15   £F
Mature yet fresh-finishing. Some elegance. Dry.

Seppelt Sparkling Shiraz 1990   16   £E
Fabulous roaring fruit.

Spar

Spar is a strange animal, fit to be exhibited centre stage at any retail museum of the twenty-second century (by which time, so I have been assured by futurologists, all shopping will be done electronically). It was created by a Dutchman at the time Sydney Harbour Bridge was first opened in the 1930s and it now spans twenty-four countries, serves 20,000 shops, and has a turnover of around eleven billion quid. Apparently the name Spar comes from the Dutch for thrift, but this is an apposite metaphor where wine is concerned in the UK only with the most basic bottles. You can pick up your £1.99 bottle of Spar Liebfraumilch, but what about more complex bargain bottles? You can judge for yourself from the list which follows.

Spar wine buying is done by the two-woman team comprising wine controller, Philippa Carr MW, and Liz Aked, wine-trading manager who came from Asda two years ago. I asked Liz to explain the difference between the world of the big supermarket and Spar.

'The nature of the beast called Spar is that it's a symbol group, so each individual retailer is a business in his own right. We communicate to the retailer through wholesalers. We've got to ensure that all our six wholesalers stock the range, have all the information, and that they pass all this on to the retailer. This is very different from the supermarket where you say, "You will have this, you will sell it at this price, you will stock it at this place on the shelf and you will have this amount of it." At Spar, it's much more about persuasion. We have to sell as well as buy, if you see what I mean.'

Sounds hard work to me. Twice as hard as a conventional wine buyer's lot.

'Well, our retailers are our greatest asset. They are the people on the shop floor who sell our wines for us.'

That means, inevitably, there are good stores and there are bad stores. Spar is a curate's egg. An individual Spar retailer is not compelled to get his wines from Philippa and Liz, and neither are the wholesalers because they're independent too. When you see the Spar sign over a doorway, it is no guarantee you'll find any of the wines I've tasted. I asked about the sort of person who buys wines at Spar.

'The general consumer has changed and become more adventurous. But the problem has been the recession. We've seen a polarization: we've seen a trading up and a trading down, and we've seen consumers who have gone back to liebfraumilch and lambrusco because they know them and they feel comfortable with them. In a recession, they don't want to waste their money on wines they don't know and understand, because it's quite a sizeable outlay. On the other hand, they've traded up to New World wines, particularly Australian, because they're getting a very good, branded package. And I think what we'll see now we're coming out of the recession is that consumers will fall away from liebfrau-milch and lambrusco again to the wines from eastern Europe and southern France. And they will continue to look at South Africa, Chile and New Zealand.

'I think the thing is,' puts in Philippa, thoughtfully, 'that Spar has got to be everything to everybody, if you like, in terms of our portfolio of products, because we've got so many different types of store. There's the neighbourhood store, there's the up-market store, there are stores which are the only store in one village, so they are serving a particular community. Then you get stores in high-street locations, or with a car park, or where people stop in on their way home from work, and those types of store tend to sell more red wines. And don't forget we're not just selling wine – we're selling a whole range of groceries and fresh foods in a microcosm.'

I'm struck by the thought that these two must be paid an awful lot of money to do wine buying under conditions like this. A couple of thousand stores each run by an idiosyncratic businessman – though some individuals own half-a-dozen shops – who can tell you to hop on yer bike if he's a mind? Humm. I asked if they managed to sneak in special-offer wines. Wines at £1.99.

'Last summer,' said Liz, 'we bought thirteen containers of liebfraumilch that we could sell at £1.99 . . .'

That's a few hundred thousand bottles.

'. . . and we sold those in two weeks.'

'I think those levels of volume,' says Philippa, 'show that Spar is potentially a major player. A sleeping giant that is only now waking up. We've got nearly 2,000 off-licences and that's a potential for serving a large number of people. And so we feel the responsibility to offer them the best value possible for a given style of wine. So we take that responsibility very seriously and we source carefully.'

I explain the problem which brings me more readers' letters than any other: non-availability of a highly recommended wine at a named store. It strikes me that at Spar there's a greater chance of running into this frustrating problem than at other retailers. Would one way of getting round this be to initiate projects of their own, like the big supermarkets do with flying wine-makers? To put company money behind wines made specially for Spar?

'Most of our stores are too small,' says Philippa, 'so the world of wine out there which has been made commercially and is available is sufficient for us to put together the range. We can physically get only a certain number of bottles on our shelves because we're fighting with petfoods, we're struggling to get shelf space from toilet rolls, or whatever, in our stores. There is a big enough variety out there for us not to need to initiate anything.'

Fighting with petfoods? An image of highly trained pitbulls pulling bottles of Mexican shiraz off the shelves and carrying them in their jaws to the waste-bin comes to mind.

'We have to tread that fine line,' she adds, 'between having an interesting range and having a slightly wacky range that people won't get to hear about and it will therefore sit on the shelves. You won't find a Mexican wine at Spar.'

I wonder how much the Spar customer is missing what is available elsewhere, but readily appreciate that if the shop-keeper balks at the idea of a particular wine, he does so because he believes he knows his customers' tastes. It's the old problem where the small grocer is concerned: he sees only the small world under his nose. These two buyers obviously believe, however, that Spar is getting somewhere with its wines, even if that somewhere isn't yet as exciting a place as it could be. Liz has the final word.

'We are developing things and I must say that, personally, I get frustrated when I read "Watch this space" and "Spar is getting there" and that sort of comment. We do sell an awful lot of wine. We have wines which are sourced from very similar places to our competitors, offering the same styles and at the same price points. We're proud of what we're doing, serving a large number of consumers and supporting a large number of retailers. It's not a question of "getting there" – we are doing the job right now. There's no point in bringing in all of these exciting wines if the retailers don't think that they can sell them, so in parallel with developing the range we're running an education programme. We're doing one-day seminars; we're giving talks and tastings. We've just finished running a New World Wine Scholarship so that retailers can learn all about New World wine. The important thing is for them to know what they've got on their shelves, because then they'll be able to sell them and serve their customers that much better.'

AUSTRALIAN WINE – *red*

Lindemans Bin 45 Cabernet Sauvignon 1991   14   £C
Soft, attractive, drinkable. Simple style, probably at its best with food rather than drunk alone. Try sausage and mash and onion gravy.

Lindemans Bin 45 Cabernet Sauvignon 1992   14   £C
Attractive berry flavours and residual richness.

Lindemans St George Vineyard Cabernet Sauvignon 1989   16   £E
Elegant, soft and smooth – an immediate fruitiness of quiet yet decidedly cassis-like concentration.

Orlando R.F. Cabernet Sauvignon 1991   16   £C
Reaches an extreme of soft yet dry-blackcurrant fruitiness with hints of spicy plum. A truly delicious wine.

St Hugo Cabernet Sauvignon 1987   14   £E
Dusty drawers and oodles of brackeny blackcurrant framing the taste of tea, with a subtle melon edging to the finish. A complex wine with a touch of tarry class.

AUSTRALIAN WINE – *white*

Lindemans Bin 65 Chardonnay 1993   16 £C
Deep, bruised fruit – lovely and ripe. Superb effect on the
tongue.

**Lindemans Cawarra, Colombard Chardonnay
1993**   14 £C
Ripe fruit character with pineapple fruit-drop acidity.
Delicious.

BULGARIAN WINE – *red*

**Bulgarian Country Wine, Merlot and Cabernet
n.v.**   10 £B
Smells like a strawberry and apple tart before being baked,
then turns into a raspberry coulis.

Korten Cabernet Sauvignon 1991   14 £B
Ripeness and dryness, blackcurrant softness.

BULGARIAN WINE – *white*

**Bulgarian Slaviantzi, Country White, Muskat and Ugni
n.v.**   13 £B
A gentle aperitif.

CHILEAN WINE – *red*

Andes Peaks Cabernet Merlot 1992   13   £C
Good soft fruit, but struggles to reach an effective climax.

CHILEAN WINE – *white*

Andes Peaks Sauvignon Blanc 1992   11   £C

FRENCH WINE – *red*

Baron Villeneuve de Cantemerle 1986   11   £E
This has a lovely bouquet, but the stalky fruit in the taste lets
it down – especially at the money. However, can you wait ten
years? If you can, the wine will be terrific.

**Cabernet Sauvignon, Vin de Pays de l'Aude
1989**   12   £B

Château Plagnac 1984   13   £D
An individual style of bordeaux with some class.

Claret 1989   10   £D
Useful size for uncritical party goers.

Claret 1992 (Spar)   14   £B
Very cheap, seriously fruity and dry claret. Good blackcurrant
fruit here. Extremely sound bargain.

Corbières 1992   10   £B

Coteaux du Languedoc n.v. (Spar) 14 £B
Excellent value. Dry, fruity, balanced – only a bit more vivacity on the finish would top it off better.

Coteaux Languedoc n.v. 13 £B
Very pleasant, easy glug. No complexity.

Côtes du Rhône, 1990 14 £A
Digestive biscuits and warm, gently toffeed fruit combine in the mouth to make this a splendid little Rhône. An outstanding bargain available in a conventional-sized bottle as well as a 50cl one – perfect for a happy solo lunch.

**Domaine Montariol, Syrah Vin de Pays d'Oc,
Domaines** 14 £B
Soft, berried fruit with a touch of fig, balanced out by vigour and bite to the acidity. Most attractive.

Fitou n.v. (Spar) 13 £B
Nothing wrong with this. Has a subtle, gamy, mushroomy undertone.

**Gamay, Vin de Pays du Jardin de la France n.v.
(Spar)** 13 £B

Julienas 1989 12 £D

Merlot Vin de Pays d'Oc 1991 11 £B

**Oaked Merlot, Vin de Pays d'Oc, Cuxac n.v.
(Spar)** 14 £C
Extremely well-structured from its reception on the tip of the tongue to clearing the back of the throat. Lots of balanced, rich fruit.

Vin de Pays de la Cité de Carcassonne 1990 14 £B
Dry, smooth, supple – with a hint of extravagance to the fruit. Great dinner-party plonk.

FRENCH WINE – *white*

Chablis, Union des Viticulteurs de Chablis
1990   13 £D
Not a bad example of the breed, but not as tightly defined as it
might be for the price.

Côtes de St-Mont, Tuilerie du Bosc 1992   14 £C
Excellent shellfish wine. Has balanced fruit and freshness.

Cuvée d'Alban, Bordeaux Blanc, Dulong 1991   12 £D

Gewürztraminer 1989   11 £C
Grand colour. Mildly spicy. Nothing eccentric. A beginner's
gewürztraminer.

Muscadet, Château des Gillières 1989   12 £C

Oaked Chardonnay, Vin de Pays d'Oc 1992
(Spar)   15 £C
Rich, oily fruit teasing out sound, ripe citric touches. Deli-
cious and very stylish. A contender with Oz!!

Reserve St-Martin Rosé de Syrah, Vin de Pays
d'Oc 1993   10 £B
Comes across like a heavily-powdered old tart, who then fails
to get excitingly fruity.

Rosé d'Anjou 1990   13 £B
A lovely-coloured rosé, but with barely a bouquet worth the
name. Yet a lovely dry, biscuity fruitiness emerges from the
taste, which is very stylish. At the price, a bargain.

Sancerre, Guy Saget 1989 and 1990   10 £E
A sancerre must be more brilliant than the '89 example to
merit the name. The '90 is better with a touch of agreeably

clean fruit, but it still lacks sufficient pedigree to wear that glorious name on its label with any pride.

Vin de Pays Du Gers n.v.   12   £B

Viognier Vin de Pays d'Oc n.v. (Spar)   15   £C
An excellent example of this uncommon grape variety from the Rhône. It has a delicious soft, almost banana-and-peach fruitiness, yet has a certain crispness of finish which belies this. An elegant, well-formed wine.

GERMAN WINE – *white*

Hock n.v.   10   £B

Mainzer Domherr, Spätlese, Müller 1992   8   £B
This is a poor spätlese. It would not make kabinett quality on some German estates. Alas, this behoves me to explain that the Germans grade their wines according to grape-ripeness levels and spätlese is supposed to result in a richer wine; but in this instance it fails to live up to its potentially exciting spätlese billing.

Niersteiner Spiegelberg Kabinett, Müller 1992   12   £C

Piesporter Goldtröpfchen Riesling QbA, Grans Fassian n.v.   14   £D
Expensive, but the fruit has a touch of lemon magic to it.

Rosenlieb 5% n.v. (Spar)   11   £B
Sweet grapes, peachy, innocuous. Good for Gran.

HUNGARIAN WINE – *red*

Danube Red n.v. (Spar)   13   £B
Some very soft, attractive fruit here.

HUNGARIAN WINE – *white*

Danube White n.v. (Spar)   12   £B

Dunavar, Prestige Chardonnay 1992   13   £C
Lacks a sufficiently rich back-up to the attractive, acidic
freshness. Maybe it'll improve in bottle over a year.

ITALIAN WINE – *red*

Barbera d'Asti, Viticoltori deli Acquese 1989   14   £C
Excellent mouth-filling stuff. Richly endowed. Superb Italian
openness and warmth.

Chianti Classico, La Canonica 1988   13   £C
A handsome, smooth Tuscan with a firm, teeth-gripping
earthiness.

Merlot del Veneto 1992 (Spar)   11   £B
Ripe black cherry, rather stalky fruit.

Valpolicella 1990   10   £B
If you like highly perfumed pear-drops in your mouth, this is
the wine for you.

ITALIAN WINE – *white*

Frascati Superiore, Colli di Catone 1989 10 £D

Pinot Grigio, Lageder 1989 12 £D

Soave 1990 14 £B
Firm, delicately toothed, clean, with a touch of citric melon –
a classic soave. And an outstanding one for the money. The
elegance of the label gives a true picture of the wine within.

Soave n.v. (Spar) 10 £B

PORTUGUESE WINE – *red*

Vinha do Monte Alentejo, 1991 15 £D
Expensive but greatly impressive. Has cherry/plum fruit
which sweetly expresses itself in the finish and sustains the
effect.

PORTUGUESE WINE – *white*

Alamo Vinho Verde n.v. (Spar) 12 £B

Duque de Viso, Dão, Sogrape 1992 13 £C
Some flavour here.

SOUTH AFRICAN WINE – *red*

Oak Village Vintage Reserve 1991   13   £C

Sable View Cabernet Sauvignon 1990   13   £C
Curious but appealing clash of fruit styles in this wine.

Table Mountain Pinot Noir 1993   12   £B
A wine of complexity, though poor varietally. This wouldn't
matter a damn if the fruit had a touch more oomph.

SOUTH AFRICAN WINE – *white*

Sable View Chardonnay 1992   15   £C
Lovely wine: full, ripe, mature yet fresh, youthful and lush.
Lots of flavour, balance and true class.

SPANISH WINE – *red*

Domino de Espinal, Yecla 1989   15   £B
Brilliant value. Mature yet richly ripe fruit with undertones of
vanilla, very soft yet dry. Terrific food wine.

Rioja n.v.   13   £C
A revelation for those who think of this wine as oaky, vanillary
and heavy. This is a young specimen and totally unaffected in
manner, nicely balanced and unhysterical. Good value.

Señorio de Nava, Ribero del Duero 1987   15   £D
Leathery fruit, dry, yet soft and mature. Has berries, woodiness and a distinct herbiness. Great roast-food and vegetable
wine.

Valencia Red n.v. (Spar)   14   £B
One of the best value reds in the land. An all-singing, all-
dancing raspberry and blackcurrant double act. Marvellous,
simple stuff.

SPANISH WINE – *white*

Valencia Dry White n.v.   12   £B
Pleasant creamy fruit under the acidity. Good value.

Valencia Medium White n.v.   11   £B

Valencia Sweet White n.v.   10   £B
Grandma, over to you.

Viña Mocen, Sauvignon Blanc Rueda 1990   13   £D
Almost gets to taste like a white Graves, but doesn't quite
make it.

SPARKLING WINE/CHAMPAGNE

Champagne Marquis de Prevel n.v. (Spar)   11   £F

Orlando Carrington Brut n.v. (Australian)   15   £D
Verve, style and value. Can't ask for more in a bottle of
bubbly.

Orlando Carrington Rosé n.v. (Australian)   13   £D

Asti Spumante n.v.   10   £D

Champagne n.v.   14   £F
A deliciously mature champagne with all the dry fruit and
calm acidity you could wish for. As good as many a *marque*'s
vintage number. Says the Spar buyer of this wine: 'It has a
very loyal following and in spite of the much-vaunted 50 per
cent drop in champagne sales in the UK, we have not noticed
any drop-off in our sales.' I must say I'm not surprised.

Moscato Fizz n.v.   10   £A
This shouldn't have a score in a wine guide because tech-
nically this wine, at 4 per cent alcohol, is not wine. It is, in
truth, partially fermented grape juice. I suppose the kids
might like it, though, and old grans, toothless from a lifetime
of chewing sugar.

Saumur Rosé, Gratien and Meyer n.v.   13   £D
A marvellously cheerful label introducing a marvellously
cheerful wine. It has, to be sure, that distinctive chenin blanc
grape variety bouquet (stale daisies), but the skins of cabernet
franc red wine grape variety – which provide the glorious
colour – give the wine body and flavour. A really stylish
champagne substitute only snobs will ignore.

Thresher

Thresher does all manner of dotty things. It is a far more eccentric organization than Oddbins – and this would, I feel, surprise most drinkers. It employs individualistic wine buyers who indulge individual passions (Jo Standen, for example, with her exclusive parcels of Château Climens, Julian Twaites with his support of the English wine industry) and these fruit pickers are shepherded by the least boring PR person in wine, who doesn't always keep her views to herself and knows a glass of wine when it's stuck under her expressive nose.

It may well be that most of the blame for Thresher's oddnesses lies at the door of Welwyn Garden City. It is a dangerous place for a head office.

Welwyn Garden City. Not every town can form a full sentence by itself. It is more swollen by an eccentric populace than Hampstead, Bath, Merseyside, Newport (Dyfed) and Arbroath combined. It must be something in the air. I have friends who live in WGC and their habits, both personal and public, make Screaming Lord Sutch appear as restrained as a church mouse.

Do you not think it odd (not to mention OTT) to hire a restaurant like Le Gavroche, as Thresher did last 16 May, to give several score wine writers a chance to stuff themselves with the most expensive food in London and to taste through ten vintages of the renowned Barsac Premier Cru Château Climens? The slim excuse of celebrating the twenty-fifth anniversary of the landing of a Russian spaceship on Venus was not mentioned once, but nothing is unlikely where Thresher is concerned. Smacking our lips through what is quaintly termed in wine buffery a 'vertical tasting', but which means, in reality, drinking standing up rather than sitting down, it was an agreeable opportunity to break away from the word-processor and while away a couple of educational hours. I learned and relearned a lot. I rediscovered how delightful it is to hear English spoken by an attractive Frenchwoman with a sexy accent while you have a glass of her home-made '91 vintage wine in your hand. I had confirmed that Barsac has its ups and downs and only in gloriously well-balanced years, as with the '91, is it a complete experience worth paying for (and most people will be better accommodated spending £3 on a bottle of Moscatel de Valencia). I feel it only fair to point out that Bottoms Up, the Thresher satellite which deals in fancy bottles, offers a six-bottle mixed case of Climens '80, '81, '82, '85, '89, and the brilliant '91 (delightful wine) for £180.

In the presence, either personally or telephonically, of Thresher's formidable PR shepherdess no negatives are admissible; thus the company is able to persuade wine writers to say yes to anything. The other satellite, Wine Rack, was last year able to call on the critical services of six cheerful grape scribes for its summer wine list and five were faithfully repre-sented, by an illustrator, in period costume, the sixth as a tropical fruit. This visual wit is somewhat tarnished, though, when the same wine list trumpets that, 'In 1988 Wine Rack was just a twinkle in a wine merchant's eye. His dream was a chain of shops with a real passion for wine, staffed by people who cared for the product and who wanted to share their enthusiasm with everyone.' I can only respond that what a pity the twinkle was not more original and the eye less green. If any chain of wine shops fits that wine merchant's dream, it is surely a major competitor who has been very visibly fulfilling its conditions for many years.

Being merely me-too, however, sits ill with Welwyn Garden Citizens. So up pops wine buyer Julian Twaites (an Old

English name, originally Norse, used in East Anglia to denote
a low meadow) to save the day with a range of English wines
so broad it borders on the lunatic. How many Bottoms Up
customers, one is surely entitled to ask, will consider forking
out £6.79 on Mersea 1992 from Colchester (in spite of its
quality)? Or £8.99 on Sharpham Barrell Fermented Dry 1992
from Devon? Obviously enough customers to make the range
a viable proposition. Some comfort is afforded by five of the
wines costing £2.99, but there is still commercial bravery in
the store's stocking so hefty a range – any one of which (there
are thirty-odd) can be ordered if the branch doesn't have a
particular bottle in stock. When I ran Julian Twaites to
ground in a pub near Twyford in Berkshire, a delightful inn
overlooking the lush low meadow of a bowling green, he was
enthusiastic and articulate: 'I took over the job of buying
English wine in March last year and inherited a tasting room
of over 150 wines. I drank as many as I could and it was very
disappointing. A lot of the wines were too old, tired, badly
made, unexciting and expensive. I then looked at the one wine
we had on our list apart from the Three Choirs Nouveau
which sadly didn't sell well, and this was the Thames Valley
Fumé for £7.99, and it was extraordinarily different, and so I
gave them a call. I looked at their entire range and I was
surprised. They were all a very different style of English wine
– fresh, lively, clean, well-balanced, good fruit and unGer-
manic. They offered something that was inherently different
to other wines in our range, but also seemed to be reasonable
value for money. So we put together a range that was available
from Thames Valley themselves and the Harvest Wine group.
They were able to provide us with samples of all the wines, so
every time a new wine went into a branch there were bottles
available for the managers, who were sceptical, to taste. The
managers got a surprise. We had about twenty-five to thirty

stores at that stage, nearly half the group, buying the wine, but still in small quantities. It wasn't until January/February this year that we started to see a big growth in distribution, new stores coming on. With the help of wine-maker John Woront-schak and marketing man Maurice Moore, we were running area meetings for Bottoms Up and then started to do some work with Wine Rack. We had managers coming down to the vineyard and often seeing a winery for the first time, seeing grapes for the first time. Our managers got more and more enthusiastic about it. We then got a full range into the ware-house, which gave us distribution to Thresher wine shops as well. We have tastings every day in Bottoms Up, two wines a day plus four or five on Saturdays. It has snowballed. From January to June this year we've shifted 15,000 cases of English wine. It's a great success. Customers are surprised about the quality of the wines. We've currently got thirty-five wines in the range, but we're going to go up to forty-five, maybe even more.'

More conventionally, Thresher also launched occasional booklets aimed at satisfying those customers posing one 'of the most frequently asked questions in a Thresher Wine Shop', which is: 'What is the best wine to go with a particular dish?' Nothing wrong with an initiative like this. I particularly liked the sections dealing with Indian food, as some of my most sublime eating experiences have come from eating this subcontinental food at one and the same time as swallowing wine, but I was sorry to read lager recommended as suitable for lamb madras (try a well-oaked red rioja or a vanillary old soak like Don Darias) and I disagree wholeheartedly with the idea of beaujolais and Indian food. Indian food will slaughter beaujolais which is, in any event, best sampled solely at wine tastings where one can avoid swallowing it. Personally, I would have thought it best in the problematical circumstances these leaflets attempt to answer to rush round to the shop with a steaming plate of the dish in question and several forks. This is certainly an option if the system of directories, indexes and codes employed in these booklets proves too demanding for any customer who has not received a thorough grounding in actuarial statistical analysis.

Thresher has also attempted to wean the weak off liebfraumilch with a range of German wines and an excellent promotional leaflet plugging them. It also has a splendid range of Alsatian wines, some very expensive but very good, and it even has a white burgundy which is not only terrific but affordable (St-Véran les Terres Noires 1993). It covers the world of wine with no significant weaknesses and some exceptional strengths (like Italian reds and New Zealand whites).

On the whole, then, much satisfaction, entertainment and agreeable wine is granted the wine drinker by virtue of Thresher's existence. Indeed, Thresher pulled off the most satisfying, entertaining and agreeable act of madness of the whole of 1994 when it became the first UK retailer to hand out free wine. This was not a mere complimentary sample in a glass in the shop while eloquent, leering assistants hover ready to lash the hesitant with honeyed tongues, but an actual free sample sachet individually packed and portable so that the customer could remove it to his own home and relish it unbuttressed. This wine was (and is) Le Cordon 1993, a red Vin de Pays d'Oc, and there is nothing else like it on the face of this earth for the technology which made it possible, after many false starts, is unique to Thresher. It is described fully on page 132.

Maybe Thresher is not so dotty after all.

AUSTRALIAN WINE – *red*

David Wynn Patriach Shiraz 1991 14 £E

Lindemans Pyrus 1988 15 £E
Lovely, subtle eucalyptus touches to the fruit – incredibly
unctuous fruit, velvet, soft, yielding.

**Lindemans St George Vineyard Cabernet
Sauvignon 1989** 16 £E
Elegant, soft and smooth – an immediate fruitiness of quiet
yet decidedly cassis-like concentration.

Moyston Cabernet/Shiraz 1992 14 £C

Penfolds Bin 35 Shiraz Cabernet 1992 15 £C
Ripe, soft fruit with some development ahead of it. Attractive
berry flavours, well-structured and balanced. Very drinkable
now, but a 17–18-pointer in three to four years.

Penfolds Bin 407 Cabernet Sauvignon 1990 16 £E
Superb specimen. Soft fruit with blackcurrant flavour in solid,
impressive form.

**Penfolds Coonawarra Cabernet Sauvignon
1990** 17 £E
The colour of crushed blackberries, subtle eucalyptus/leather
aroma, sheer-satiny acids and velvet-textured fruit touches –
lovely tannicky finish.

**Redcliffs Coonawarra Cabernet Sauvignon
1991** 14 £C

Riddoch Coonawarra Cabernet Shiraz 1990 15 £D
Polished, complex, ripe.

Tollana Cabernet Sauvignon, SE Australia 1991   14   £C

Tollana Cabernet/Shiraz 1992   13   £C

Tollana Red n.v.   14   £B
Ripe, rich fruit.

AUSTRALIAN WINE – *white*

Bridgewater Mill Riesling 1993   14   £C
Attractive, but a curious expression of the grape.

Cape Mentelle Chardonnay 1992   17   £E
Buttered lemons and nuts undercut by a gentle melon fruit.
Superb elegance and style.

Chapel Hill Riesling 1993   11   £D

Katnook Estate Coonawarra Sauvignon Blanc
1993   12   £E
A cat got in among the fruit too – and peed a little.

Lindemans Bin 65 Chardonnay 1993   16   £C
Deep, bruised fruit – lovely and ripe. Superb effect on the tongue.

Lindemans Padthaway Chardonnay 1992   15   £E
A somewhat quiet chardonnay for an Aussie, but don't mistake
the purity of the fruit or the keenness of purpose.

Oxford Landing Chardonnay 1993   14   £C
Works well, the fruit and acid. Good balance.

Oxford Landing Sauvignon Blanc 1993   14   £C
Impressive: good fruit, acid, style and great with fish (like
grilled sole).

Penfolds Bin 21 Semillon/Chardonnay 1993   15   £C
Fresh and lively, yet a dollop of pineappley melon keeps intruding. Delicious refreshing wine.

**Penfolds Bin 202 South Australian Riesling
1993**   14   £C
Superb, rich aperitif. Delicious.

Penfolds Koonunga Hill Chardonnay 1992   14   £C
Full, lush fruit plus a ticklish dollop of lemon zest. Delicious, but getting pricey near a fiver.

Penfolds Semillon/Chardonnay 1993   14   £C
Excellent recipe: fruit, acid, wood but will integrate and improve mightily over the next one to two years.

Penfolds South Australia Chardonnay 1992   16   £D
Lovely, polished, lush, woody fruit with touches of lemon, beautifully balanced. Elegant – a real alternative, at a far lower price, to fine burgundy.

Petaluma Chardonnay 1991   16   £E
Stylish, big, full, yet it has balance – rather like seeing a muscle man on a tightrope.

Riddoch Chardonnay 1991   15   £D
Oily, ripe, full (not overblown), very satisfying. Great with spicy grilled chicken and oriental food.

Riddoch Riesling 1993   13   £C

St Hallet Chardonnay 1992   17   £E
Plays with both hands on the piano, all the notes in place: beautiful integration of fruit and wood. Superb! Delicious!

Taltarn Sauvignon Blanc 1992   12   £D

Tollana Chardonnay 1993   13   £C
Chewy, sunny fruit, a mite on the pricey side.

Tollana Coonawarra Riesling 1993   13   £C
Attractive aperitiff.

Tollana Dry 1993   12   £B

Tollana MacLaren Vale Oak Aged Chardonnay
1993   15   £C
Lots of rich, swirling fruit. Stylish, full, great with roast chicken.

Tollana Medium Dry White 1993   13   £B
More interesting fruit than the dry version.

Tollana Semillon/Chardonnay 1993   12   £C
Bananas with pineapples merrily clanging.

Tyrrells 'Old Winery' Chardonnay 1992   15   £D
Nice one, Bruce baby. Very quiet and stylish, with all the fruit
we've come to love in Hunter Valley chardonnays, but a soft
touch with it too.

Wynn's Coonawarra Riesling 1993   14   £C
Ripe, balanced wine to enjoy by itself.

BULGARIAN WINE – *red*

Cabernet Sauvignon, Pulden 1989   13   £B

Vintage Premier Cabernet Sauvignon 1993   14   £B

Vintage Premier Merlot 1993   15   £B
Bargain fruit. Some serious dry touches to a lovely, rounded
depth of flavour. Excellent with cheeses.

BULGARIAN WINE – *white*

Khan Krum Chardonnay 1990 12 £C

Slaviantzi Country Wine n.v. 9 £B
Try it behind your ears.

CHILEAN WINE – *red*

Caliterra Reserva Cabernet Sauvignon 1992 16 £D
Red, smooth, deliciously soft, berried fruit with an engaging,
rich, meaty edge. This edge is subtle but persistent. An
elegant wine which makes every concession to be liked. Available in Wine Rack and Bottoms Up stores.

Chilean Cabernet Sauvignon n.v. 12 £C
Biscuity, chewy fruit.

Las Colinas n.v. 14 £B
Delightful little wine with perky fruit, good balance and effective tannic styling. Excellent with food (roasts, etc.).

Las Colinas Merlot/Cabernet Sauvignon 1993 14 £C
Solid yet free of any hardness, smooth and fruity. Basic, but
very drinkable – especially with simple meat dishes.

CHILEAN WINE – *white*

Errazuriz Sauvignon Blanc 1993 16 £C
Deep, serious, full of style and flavour. Great fruit and

balance. Classy in feel, not pricey in fact.

Las Colinas Chilean White 1993   15   £B
Brilliant price for a superbly well-constructed mouthful of
fruit – richly edged and full, without being blowsy.

Las Colinas Sauvignon/Semillon 1994   15   £C
Superb double act of grape varieties singing softly and deliciously together. Great summer drinking with fruit, acid and
overall pleasing zippiness.

Santa Carolina Gran Reserva Chardonnay 1993 16   £E
Rich, slightly exotic, complex, serious, fun, compelling.
Pricey, but worth it.

**Santa Carolina Special Reserve Sauvignon Blanc
1993**   14   £D
Great stuff. Exceptional.

ENGLISH WINE – *white*

Heritage Fumé 1992   16   £D
A strikingly clean and elegant English wine of considerable
class. It sits, deliciously, between the sancerre of old and New
Zealand sauvignon blancs of the 1990s. Available at Thresher
group stores only.

Mersea 1992   14   £D
Well structured from start to finish, with nice ortega (grape
variety) richness showing through on the fruit. Available at
Bottoms Up stores.

Moorlynch Estate Selection 1992   11   £D
Grapefruit on the nose leads to some soft fruit on the middle

palate. But what fruit this wine has, has a bland quality.
Available at Bottoms Up stores.

Northbrook Springs Medium Dry 1992   12   £D
Expensive for the sweet fruit on offer. Available at Bottoms Up
stores.

Pilton Manor Dry Reserve 1991   12   £D
A bit muddy on the front and a bit short on the finish. Rather
expensive for the fruit on offer. Available at Bottoms Up stores.

Sharpham Barrel Fermented Dry 1993   13   £E
Very attractive grapefruit and ginger fruit, and well-structured,
but over-priced for the quality of fruit on offer. Available at
Bottoms Up stores.

Sharpham Estate Reserve 1992   12   £D
Really ripe fruit finishes on a sour, rather bitter note. A touch
overdone. Available at Bottoms Up stores.

Sharpham Estate Selection 1992   12   £D
Gingery nose and fruit which has some richness. Available at
Bottoms Up stores.

Valley Vineyards Fumé 1992   16   £E
Beautiful, elegant, stylish and clean with lovely fruit and a good
structure. Will age well too. Available at Bottoms Up stores.

Valley Vineyards Hinton Grove 1992   14   £D
Attractive 'off-dry' wine with pleasantly rounded, soft fruit.
Available at Bottoms Up stores.

Valley Vineyards Regatta 1992   13   £D
This wine has a minerally character, some weight of fruit and a
balanced structure. In short, it is well made – very clean.
Available at Bottoms Up stores.

Wickham Fumé 1992   15   £D
Lovely style of fruit, clean, fresh and gently nutty. This wine's
available at the House of Commons bar and I hope MPs
choke on it, considering the unfair duty levels English wine-
makers are forced to swallow. Available at Bottoms Up stores.

Wickham Vintage Selection Dry 1993   13   £D
A delicate, attractive nose leads to ripe fruit and some weight
on the finish. Good structure. Available at Bottoms Up stores.

FRENCH WINE – *red*

Berloup St-Chinian 1991   11   £C

Château Bonnet, Reserve André Lurton 1990   15   £D
Excellent value with its dry, yet soft style.

Château Coucheroy, Pessac-Leognan 1990   16   £D
A great wine for the money. True class and style.

Château d'Arsuc, Haut-Médoc 1990   15   £E
Superbly structured aromatic fruit.

Château de Francs, Cote de Francs 1989   15   £E
Excellent stuff. Real, deep fruit, dry, potent.

Château de la Liquière, Faugères n.v.   14   £C
Growls with flavour, comforting one on a cold night in front of
the telly.

**Château de Lastours, Corbières Cuvée Descamps
1990**   13   £D
Very deep and rich.

Château de Lastours, Corbières 1989   13   £D
Some agreeable fruit here, rich and dry. Good with roast foods.

Château de Laurens Faugères 1992   16   £C
This is so soft you can't at first believe it. It would be easier to catch a cloud in your hands than it would be to catch any evidence of tannins or harshness in this slippery beauty. It's all soft fruit, faintly meaty at the edges. Great picnic wine.

Château de Violet, Minervois 1992   13   £D
Soft, ripe plums.

Château Guibon, Bordeaux AC 1992   14   £C
Rich, authentic, very delicious.

Château Les Ollieux Romanis, Corbières 1990   12   £C

Château Manon La Lagune, Premières Côtes de Blaye n.v.   10   £C

Château Ramage La Batisse, Haut-Médoc 1989   15   £E
Cedary class. The real thing.

Château Rosé d'Orion, Montagne St-Émilion 1991   14   £C

Château St-Auriol, Corbières 1992   14   £D
Soft, deep, velvety, balanced and classy.

Château St-Estève Côtes du Rhone 1991   13   £C

Claret n.v.   12   £C

Claret Bordeaux Supérieur 1991   12   £C

Corbières l'Estagnon 1991   12   £B

Côtes de Nuits Villages, Domaine d'Arlot Clos du Chapeau 1991   12   £F
Some hints at striving to make a burgundy here. But what a price!

Côtes du Rhone 1993, Viognier   11   £D

Côtes du Rhône J. P. Bartier 1992   11   £C

Crozes-Hermitage Domaine Barret 1992   11   £D

Cuvée Pierre Sicard, Minervois 1991   12   £C

Domaine Barmes Syrah, Coteaux du Languedoc 1992   12   £C
Dank, rich fruit requires dank, rich food.

Domaine Barthes 1992   12   £C
A 100 per cent syrah wine which is a touch too expensive for the style on offer; dry, some rich fruit, rather plain and trim.

Domaine de la Rectorie, Banyuls 1993   14   £D
A red pud wine? Yes. And no. Try it with fruit and cheese.

Domaine de Montine Coteaux du Tricastin 1992   12   £C

Domaine de Rivoyre Cabernet Sauvignon 1992   14   £C
Blackberry/cherry. Amusing, diminutive, cheeky.

Domaine du Grand Bosc, Fitou 1991   11   £C

Domaine Gauby Côtes du Roussillon 1991   13   £D
Good, rich-edged fruit.

Domaine Ste-Eulalie, Minervois 1992   11   £C

Fitou, Mme Claude Parmentier n.v.   10   £C

Fleurie, Cellier de Samsons 1992   10   £D

Graves, P. Coste 1990	12	£C

L'Estagnon Rouge n.v.	13	£B

Le Cordon Lot 37 1993	14	£C

Le Cordon rouge, in the form it was given to me, is a breakthrough – a first for Thresher. There is nothing else like it on the face of this earth and there are two reasons for this. First, the wine is packaged in one of those sachets which hold the ketchup in motorway cafeterias and second, it costs nothing to acquire. Stroll into any Thresher shop and they'll give you the wine, a decent gluggable amount, for nowt. In other words, it is a free sample. Personally I think Concorde would have been a better name: the sachet is a technological breakthrough and surely it will fly out of the shops. However, the question must be asked: is it worth buying the bottle? The sachet rates 20 points, for surely wine you can take out of the shop for free (if it is as drinkable as Le Cordon) rates the highest, but the bottle at £3.99 rates 14 points. It is dry, wryly plummy with some serious richness, and it is very well-balanced; but the beauty of it is you can find all this out for yourself without putting your hand in your pocket. Indeed, if Thresher extends the idea to all its bottles there is hardly any need for wine writers like me and I dare say there's many a retailer, not to mention wine-maker, who will shout amen to that.

Mâcon-Bray Domaine de la Combe 1991	10	£D

Mâcon Rouge, Jean-Paul Bartier 1993	10	£C

Mature Claret n.v.	12	£C

Momtus, Madiran 1990	13	£E

This is a very attractive, rich wine at a not-very-attractive, rich price.

Pinot Noir Joseph de Belair Vin de Pays d'Oc 1992   4   £C
With a smell like drying cement mixed with drawer dust, this is
not a hugely appealing wine. The fruit is as meagre as a gnat's
breakfast.

Rasteau, La Ramillade 1990   15   £D
Delicious, rich fruit.

Sablet, La Ramillade 1991   14   £D

Sauvigny les Beaune 1990   10   £E
Perfectly drinkable – reluctant raspberry fruit – but dull beyond
belief for the price.

Sirius Red n.v.   10   £D
Some weight of fruit, but rather disappointing structure. Some
aroma, too, but ill-defined. A formula wine made to a recipe,
like tinned food.

**St-Amour, Domaine de la Pirolette Georges
Duboeuf   10   £D**

St-Joseph l'Olnaie 1991   14   £F
Smells like pinot, tastes like herby tar.

Terroir du Tuchan, Fitou 1991   11   £E

Vacqueras Domaine Le Couroulu 1989   12   £D

Val du Torgan n.v.   14   £B
Rich, slightly hairy fruit. Earthy, and has pretensions to
robustness.

Valerianes Vin de Pays de Vaucluse 1992   13   £B

Vin de Pays des Coyeaux de Peyriac 1993   14   £B
Hammy, dry, plummy, light, cheap. It is rated as a light wine
and deserves its rating, but it is not heavy with fruit or complex.

FRENCH WINE – *white*

Alsace Tradition Turckheim 1992   12   £C
Pleasant, but not hugely 'together' or purposeful.

Bordeaux Blanc 1993   11   £B

Bordeaux Sauvignon 1993   13   £C
Some attractive fruit here.

Chablis Louis Alexandre 1993   10   £D

Chablis Premier Cru Beauroy 1992   13   £E

Chardonnay Vin de Pays d'Oc 1993   13   £B

Château Bonnet Entre-Deux-Mers 1992   12   £C

Château Bonnet Entre-Deux-Mers Oak Aged 1991   13   £E
Classy fruit, but expensive.

Château de Coucheroy 1992   14   £D
Like it, don't love it (not at six quid), but I do like it.

Château de la Jaubertie Sauvignon 1993   14   £C
A highly drinkable rosé.

Château de Rovergue 1992   11   £C

Domaine de l'Hortus Rosé 1993   12   £C

Figaro Vin de Pays de l'Herault 1993   10   £B

Gewürztraminer Grand Cru, Brand 1990   14   £F
Delicious, but expensive.

Le Cordon 1993   13   £C

Menetou-Salon Morogues 1992   13 £D
Rich fruit, not hugely fresh or typical.

Mouton Cadet 1992   10 £D
Barely recommendable. And what a cheek at the price.

Muscadet 1993   10 £C

Muscadet Château de la Cornillière 1993   13 £C
Some fine fruit on display here.

Petit Chablis Château de Maligny 1992   11 £E

Petit Chablis Goulley 1992   11 £D

Pouilly-Fuissé 1993   11 £D

Pouilly-Fumé des Duchesses 1993   13 £E

Premier Côtes de Bordeaux AC n.v.   12 £C
Pud wine.

Riesling Ollwiller 1990, Turckheim   11 £E

Riesling Trimbach 1989, Cuvée Frederic Emile   12 £G

Riesling Vieilles Vignes Blanck 1989   10 £F
Lemon juice.

Rivesaltes Vieille Reserve 1980   12 £D
Raisiny and sweet.

Rosé de Cabernet Sauvignon 1993   12 £C

Sauvignon Dom des Salices 1993   13 £C
Some real sauvignon character here.

Sauvignon La Chapeut 1993   14 £C
Excellent fruit. Balanced.

Sauvignon Touraine La Chapelle de Cray 1993   15   £C
A class act. A bit restrained on the fruit for those used to New
Zealand, but this example is in good voice nevertheless. Has a
crispness of attack which is deeply delicious – and good news
for shellfish marriage brokers.

Sirius White   9   £D
Serious woody nose. Sticky fruit with acid all out of kilter.
Weedy finish. Expensive crap.

St-Joseph 1992, Pierre Coursodon   12   £E

St-Véran Georges Duboeuf 1992   13   £C

St-Véran Les Terres Noires 1993   15   £E
Superb rich fruit. Full of style and flavour. At last! A white
burgundy really worth the money.

Touraine Sauvignon Domaine des Duchesses
1993   13   £E

Vin de Pays du Gers, Au Loubet 1993   13   £B
Lush fruit and acidity. Good value.

Vouvray Champalou 1992   12   £D

White Burgundy 1993   10   £C

Zind Humbrecht Tokay Pinot Gris Vieilles
Vignes 1991   15   £G
Vivid apricot fruit.

GERMAN WINE – *white*

Deinhard Riesling Dry 1991   10   £D

Dr Loosen Riesling 1992   15   £D
Keep for three to four years, but if you must drink it now, chill
it and serve with smoked salmon.

Dr Loosen Riesling Kabinett 1992   16   £D
Real sherbet lime undercutting the fruit. Superb aperitif.

Kreuznacher Brucken Riesling Auslese 1989   9   £E
Fair tears the teeth out, the acidity. Lay down for at least 250
years.

Niersteiner Gutes Domtal 1993   13   £C

HUNGARIAN WINE – *red*

Villany Hills Cabernet Sauvignon 1992   15   £B
Touch of leather on the bouquet, rich fruit, dry and brambly
to the tongue, with good balancing acidity and a firm finish.
Excellent value for money. Has soft but noticeable tannins
which impart a pleasant grip to the wine and I dare say the
wine would age well for a couple of years. Excellent roast and
grilled-food wine.

Villany Hills Merlot 1992   12   £B
Some spiciness about the fruit.

HUNGARIAN WINE – *white*

Hungarian Muscat 1991   13   £B
A delicious, light aperitif. Has musky, spicy, dry-elderberry
overtones.

Muscat 1993 13 £B
Interesting aperitif.

Pinot Blanc 1992 12 £B

ITALIAN WINE – *red*

Barco Reale 1993 13 £D

Chianti Ruffina Selvapiana 1990 15 £D
A pedigree red wine which offers you options. You can put the
wine down for some years, maybe five or six, and achieve a
superior, earthy softness with deeper berried fruits, or you can
drink it now and enjoy a brisker style of fruit with a hint of
pepper. I must confess I knocked it back, after letting it
breathe for a couple of hours, and felt the future could take
care of itself.

Chianti Ruffina Grati 1991 13 £C

Le Volte 1992 12 £E
Attractive, but overpriced. Available in Wine Rack and Bottoms Up.

Merlot, Friuli-Grave 1993 12 £B
Light, with some fruit.

Parrina 1991 11 £C

Rosso Piceno, Umani Ronchi 1992 12 £C

Salice Salentino Riserva, Taurino 1990 14 £C
Mature fruit with hints of earth.

ITALIAN WINE – *white*

Argiolas Bianco di Sardegna 1992   13   £E
Delicious, but expensive.

Arneis Castello di Neive 1992   10   £D

Bardolino Chiaretto n.v.   13   £B
Light and fresh and pleasantly cherryish.

Bianco di Custoza 1992   14   £C
Delicious zip here.

Ca dei Frati Lugana 1992   14   £D
Nutty, lemony, delicious with shellfish.

Chardonnay del Salento 1993   10   £C

Gewürztraminer Alto Adige 1992   10   £C

I Capitelli Recioto di Soave 1991 (half-bottle)   17   £E
Complex wine of huge appeal to hard-fruit tart eaters: nuts,
raisins, apricots and creamy peaches. Has huge length and
wonderful after-taste.

Tocai del Veneto 1993   12   £B

Vernaccia di San Gimignano 1992   11   £C

Vernaccia di San Gimignano 1992 Riserva   12   £D

MOLDOVAN WINE – *red*

Rochu de Hincesti 1992   14   £B
Cheering, burnt cherry/plum fruit. Pleasantly dry.

MOLDOVAN WINE – *white*

Rkatsiteli n.v.   14   £B
Lemon zesty wine of great charm.

Sauvignon n.v.   12   £B

NEW ZEALAND WINE – *white*

Collards Alan Gunn Chardonnay 1992   15   £E
Superb rich fruit.

Cook's Bay Chardonnay 1992   15   £D
Ripe and lush, keen and fresh. Excellent.

Cook's Gisborne Sauvignon Blanc 1992   13   £D

Esk Valley Rosé 1993   15   £C
Brilliant cherry fruit. Fresh and fruity, yet really stylish and
not merely a pink punk.

Gisborne Dry White, Kapua Springs n.v.   14   £C
One of those 100 per cent müller-thurgau wines, demons-
trating how much pleasant fruit can be coaxed out of this
grape variety when it's handled right.

Hunter's Chardonnay 1991   14   £E
Bright and ripe, finishes lightly.

Hunter's Sauvignon Blanc 1993   15   £E
Balanced, sane, very pure and clean. Preaches fruit without
screaming it.

Jackson Estate Sauvignon Blanc 1993,
Marlborough   16   £E
Not huge grassiness here, just gentle, soothing fruit and
balanced stylishness. One of the most elegantly purposeful of
sauvignon blancs around. Will repay cellaring for two to three
years. Very fine.

Kapua Springs Dry White 1993   14   £C
Bargain freshness and flavour. Delicious.

Matua Valley, Judd Estate Chardonnay 1991   14   £E
Has some beautiful touches up front, but doesn't quite, by a
smidgin, finish with the same flourish.

Montana Sauvignon Blanc 1993   14   £C
Pleasant working herbaceous acidity. Marvellous with shellfish.

Morton Estate Hawkes Bay Chardonnay 1991   16   £D
Superb, rich, sophisticated fruit. Rolls around the mouth like
pearls.

Palliser Estate Chardonnay 1992   16   £E
Lovely touches of oily wood on the soft fruit which finishes
firmly and lengthily.

Stoneleigh Sauvignon Blanc 1993   13   £D

Stoneleigh Vineyard Riesling 1993   13   £C
Interesting cosmetic edge to the fruit.

Timara Medium Dry White 1993   13   £C
A soft and gentle introduction to New Zealand.

Vidal Merlot Rosé 1993   16   £D
Probably the highest scoring rosé ever. Has richness, flavour,
yet it's not full or overripe – nor is it too frivolous. It's a serious
rosé with seriously delicious fruit.

Vidal Sauvignon 1992　　　　　　　　14　£D
Ripe, rich fruit, not aggressively packaged.

Villa Maria Riesling 1993　　　　　　13　£D
Excellent aperitif.

Villa Maria Sauvignon Blanc 1993　　15　£D
They always get enough lift from the fruit here to balance out
the grassy acids. Superb.

Wairau River Chardonnay 1992　　　　14　£E

Wairau River Sauvignon Blanc 1993　　14　£E
Delicious; expensive.

PORTUGUESE WINE – *red*

Alandra, Hordade do Esporão n.v.　　15　£B
Floral notes to a dry wine which is robustly capable (although
it is not a hugely rich wine) of tackling spicy food.

Bairrada Reserve Dom Ferraz 1989　　13　£B

Beira Mar Garrafeira 1980　　　　　15　£D
This belies its age with fruit so unwrinkled it's incredible. The
Joan Collins of Portuguese wine.

Charter LBV Port 1987　　　　　　13　£E

Dom Ferraz Reserva, Barraida 1989　　13　£B

Dom Ferraz Reserva, Dão 1989　　　14　£B

Meia Pipa J. P. Vinhos Reserva 1988　14　£C
Compelling bouquet, good fruit.

Quinta de Lamelas Douro 1992   16   £C
Has a wonderful finishing edge of figgy liquorice.

Ramada n.v.   15   £B
Cherries and raspberries drily expressed. Soft, creamy touch
to this fruit. Delightful quaffing wine.

Ramada Vinho de Mesa n.v.   11   £B

Skeffington 1977 **Vintage Port**   13   £G

PORTUGUESE WINE – *white*

Albis 1992   12   £C

Cartuxa 1991   14   £D
Firm and delicious. Superb with grilled mackerel with mus-
tard butter.

Cova da Ursa Chardonnay 1991   13   £E

Dom Ferraz Reserva, Barraida 1993   13   £B

Palo do Cordido Vinho Verde 1992   11   £D

Quinta de Paulas n.v.   15   £C
Toasted sesame-seed aroma plus a distant smokiness and
gaminess like a good white burgundy. The fruit is pleasantly
Continental, seems about to go somewhere hugely exciting
but then to pull up. But it is very enjoyable.

Ramada n.v.   14   £B
Modest, fresh, pear-drop fruit, slightly fat, almost baked fruit.
Good structure and build. Brilliant value.

SLOVAKIAN WINE – *red*

St Laurent, Slovakia n.v.   12   £B

SLOVAKIAN WINE – *white*

Gruner Veltliner n.v.   11   £B

SOUTH AFRICAN WINE – *red*

Blue Ridge Rouge, Villiera Estate 1993   14   £C
Spicy, soft, deep, rich. A serious wine without a serious price
tag. Has an excellent food-sympathetic, savoury tang on the
finish.

Cavendish Port LBV 1963   15   £D
A hugely caramel and sticky-toffee wine, which with Xmas
pud aflame might prove rather fine.

Kanonkop Pinotage 1991   16   £E
Cough-mixture thick, very dry, huge burnt-cassis finish.
Expensive, but potent company. (Good with cheeses.) Avail-
able at Bottoms Up only.

Merlot, Villiera Estate 1993   15   £D
Ripe and dry, full, extremely deep and rich edged. A very
companionable bottle for cheeses and roast meats.

SOUTH AFRICAN WINE – *white*

De Wetshof Chardonnay d'Honneur 1993   16   £D
Deliciously demure and ripe fruit in a subtle, classy, woody
way. Exceptionally well-balanced, nutty, fruity wine.

KWV Chenin Blanc 1993   13   £C
Some attractive rich fruit here.

KWV Sauvignon Blanc 1993   12   £C

Muscat d'Alexandrie 1993   11   £B
Mildly amusing.

Winelands Chenin Blanc 1993   14   £B
Bright and breezy, delicious with its typically South African,
pear-drop-edged tropical fruit and great freshness.

Winelands Medium Dry White 1993   13   £B
Very accommodating drinking for those who like a touch of
mellow, soft sweetness with their fruit.

Winelands Muscat d'Alexandrie 1993   13   £B
A lovely ripe aperitif.

SPANISH WINE – *red*

Albor Campo Viejo 1992   14   £C

Baron de Lay Rioja Reserva 1987   15   £D

Campo Viejo Reserva Rioja 1988   15   £C
Not overblown or too woody. Elegant, richly restrained.

Conde de Valdemar Reserva Rioja 1987	15	£D

Conde de Valdemar Rioja Crianza 1989	16	£C

Soft, ripe, really digs its heels in fruit-wise. Excellent.

Contino Reserva Rioja 1986	13	£E

Copa Real n.v.	14	£B

Domino de Espinal Yecla 1989	14	£B

Has some character to it, but suggests it is the product of high-yielding vines. Little flair to it, but enough taste to score well. Woody fruit, soft, not berried. Rather thin to finish, but attractive to the nose and the palate without rich food. Good value plonking for a bookworm or a stereo-music lover.

Don Darias n.v.	14	£B

You know how sometimes you meet an upfront, fruity person whose ribald sense of humour almost makes you blush, but you can't help yourself falling completely under his or her spell? So it is with this wine.

Don Domingo n.v.	14	£B

Thresher's Don Domingo (nominally a Sunday wine, but it lacks the weight to handle a hefty sabbath nosh-up) is declassified red rioja and is all the better for its failure to be officially esteemed by the Spanish authorities, otherwise it would cost a good deal more than £2.79. It has the typical vanilla and banana aroma and flavouring to the soft fruit, but these toothsome qualities are more acorn than full-blown oak – as would be experienced from 'proper' riojas. A friendly, undemanding tipple, Don Domingo easily rates 14 points and is available at all Thresher's various enterprises including Wine Rack and Bottoms Up. You will recognize the bottle by the totally sozzled nonagenarian on the label. This glorious testament to rustic rousting wears a floppy straw hat, a droopy moustache and an expression of beatific smugness, which can only have been bequeathed by his consumption of at least five full bottles of the wine.

Santara 1993   14   £B
Seriously good, right-on fruit. Dry, full, rich, yet very quaffable. A great pasta wine.

Señorio de Sarria, Cabernet Sauvignon Navarra 1987   14   £D
Expensive, but full of fruit.

Valencia Red n.v.   14   £B
Simple, soft, fruity, with enough dry finish to invite a second glass.

Vega Camelia, Rioja 1992   15   £B
Light, flouncy rioja with hints of soft, vanilla berries.

Viña Albali Reserva, Valdepeñas 1987   15   £C
Creamy, touch of vanilla. Delicious.

Viña Mayor, Ribera del Duero 1991   13   £C

SPANISH WINE – *white*

Casal da Barca Ribeiro 1992   13   £B
Delicious fish wine.

Copa Real n.v.   13   £B
Zip and fruit. Good value.

Copa Real Rosado n.v.   14   £B
Dry yet fresh. Has fruit and style.

| **Marqués de Murietta Rioja 1987** | 12 | £E |

Fine with spicy food, not so without.

| **Valdemar Rioja 1993** | 12 | £B |

| **Valdemar Rosado 1993 Rioja** | 14 | £C |

Fresh yet fruity. Excellent.

USA WINE – *white*

| **Chalk Hill Chardonnay 1991** | 13 | £F |

| **Chalk Hill Sauvignon Blanc 1991** | 15 | £E |

Lovely fruit style.

| **Kah-Nock-Tie Sauvignon Blanc 1992** | 14 | £D |

Delicious – pricey, but delicious.

| **Newtonian Chardonnay 1992** | 13 | £E |

Not as overwhelmingly great as I thought it would be, with the burgeoning reputation of this vineyard. The style is quiet (so quiet it is certainly a chardonnay for those drinkers who say they dislike New World oaked chardonnays) and whisperingly impressive. But without food it lacks the complexity or weight to combat the price.

SPARKLING WINE/CHAMPAGNE

| **Cattier Premier Cru Champagne n.v.** | 13 | £G |
| **Chassenay Champagne n.v.** | 13 | £F |

Hamm Reserve Premier Cru Champagne n.v.   13   £G

Jean de Praisac Champagne n.v.   12   £F

Le Mesnil Blanc de Blancs, Champagne n.v.   14   £G
Mature, stylish champagne.

Montoy Brut Champagne n.v.   12   £F

**Seaview Pinot Noir/Chardonnay 1990
(Australian)**   15   £E
Mature, fruity, classy. Great value.

Segura Viudas Brut Riserva n.v. (Cava)   13   £D

Seppelt Blanc de Blancs Brut 1990 (Australia)   13   £E
Solid, dependable, gently citric bubbly.

Seppelt Great Western Brut n.v. (Australia)   16   £C
Superb bargain. A finer fizzer on sale for under a fiver it's
difficult to name. Lemony, zingy, zesty. Great style.

Seppelt Great Western Rosé n.v.   15   £D

**Seppelt Pinot Chardonnay Brut 1989
(Australia)**   16   £E
Really deep and throaty, yet gently lemonic. A superb tonic
for tired taste-buds. Brilliant.

**Seppelt Salinger Sparkling Wine n.v.
(Australia)**   15   £F
Mature, yet fresh finishing. Some elegance. Dry.

Unwins

I guessed the quartet of pros who greeted me as I entered the tasting room were red-wine fanciers. And I was right. Professional wine-buying is one of the most difficult purchasing areas in which to remain professionally objective, and it struck me that these chaps liked their red wine and regarded white merely as something on which to warm up. They'd have trouble finding unusual, delicate whites, apart from the usual lot you'd expect to find, like a sound Alsatian pinot blanc, or a Gyongyos chardonnay, I guessed, and I discovered little to disabuse me of my first impression. The unusual white Buzet was an exception, though, and so was the Vaucheron Sancerre at nigh-on a tenner.

At Unwins, then, Senator McCarthy's nightmare has come true. The place is overrun by reds. I found deeply committed examples wherever I turned. Unwins is a privately owned chain of 300 shops concentrated in the south-east of England and East Anglia, and these establishments come across as the type of garish off-licences, also catering to chocoholics and crisp snackers, into which the Oddbins *aficionado*, for example, would not be seen dead or even dying. May I invite such drinkers to reconsider their route as they wend their dignified way to the grave?

Château Mingot Côtes de Castillon 1990, for example, is seriously dry and deliciously rich. It is a very well-constructed wine, with that touch of suede-textured meatiness to the rugged fruit the Castillon wines exhibit as their general characteristic. Domaine de Caunettes Hautes, Cabardes 1989, is also a perfectly mature wine, but it's from the south with deep, penetrating, smoothly achieved bordeaux-type fruit

of some class. The cheapest drinkable red in the place, however, comes from La Mancha and goes by that name. It costs
£1.99 at the time of drinking.

For a lot of drinkers, mostly the occasional ones, Unwins is
a safe place to buy wine. You know where you are with the
bloke behind the counter because he's as down to earth and
no-nonsense as you are.

The perfect place to find the odd little bargain beauty. Help
yourself from the list which follows.

AUSTRALIAN WINE – *red*

Lindemans Bin 45 Cabernet Sauvignon 1992   14   £C
Attractive berry flavours and residual richness.

Lindemans Cabernet Sauvignon Bin 45 1991   14   £C
At its peak of drinkability. Rich and flavourful.

**Lindemans St George Vineyard Cabernet
Sauvignon 1989**   16   £E
Elegant, soft and smooth – an immediate fruitiness of quiet
yet decidedly cassis-like concentration.

Penfolds Bin 35 Shiraz Cabernet 1992   15   £C
Ripe, soft fruit with some development ahead of it. Attractive
berry flavours, well-structured and balanced. Very drinkable
now, but a 17–18-pointer in three to four years.

Stockman's Bridge n.v.   14   £C
Simple and delicious. Excellent with pasta.

AUSTRALIAN WINE – *white*

Lauriston Rhine Riesling 1991 Adelaide Hills   12   £E

**Lindemans Chardonnay Bin 65 1993, SE
Australia**   15   £C
Lots of rich, buttery fruit, richly spread on the acidity. Great
stuff.

Penfolds Bin 21 Semillon/Chardonnay 1993   15   £C
Fresh and lively, yet a dollop of pineappley melon keeps
intruding. Delicious, refreshing wine.

Penfolds Koonunga Hill Chardonnay 1992   14   £C
Full, lush fruit plus a ticklish dollop of lemon zest. Delicious,
but getting pricey near a fiver.

Penfolds Semillon/Chardonnay 1993   14   £C
Excellent recipe: fruit, acid, wood but will integrate and
improve mightily over the next one to two years.

Penfolds South Australia Chardonnay 1992   16   £D
Lovely polished, lush, woody fruit with touches of lemon,
beautifully balanced. Elegant – a real alternative, at a far lower
price, to fine burgundy.

Stockman's Bridge n.v.   13   £C
Has fruit; can't be faulted on fruit.

**Wakefield White Clare Crouchen-Chardonnay
1989, Clare**   16   £C
Resounds with all sorts of fruits, soft and ripe, underripe, tart,
rich and delicious. Has a curiously delicious, ripe richness.
Great with spicy oriental food.

AUSTRIAN WINE – *red*

Blauer Zweigelt 1992 14 £C
Light, hugely appealing, supple fruit – cherries and plums.
Delicious chilled.

AUSTRIAN WINE – *white*

Eiswein 1991 Neusidlersee Burgenland 13 £E
Wonderful with peaches and ice-cream.

Gruner Veltliner 1993 14 £C
As delicious as ever.

BULGARIAN WINE – *red*

Merlot Reserve 1988 Stambolovo Region 13 £C
Do they stick mint leaves in with the grapes when they crush
them? Curious wine, but hugely drinkable.

CHILEAN WINE – *red*

Canepa Cabernet Sauvignon 1993 Maipo Valley 13 £C

CHILEAN WINE – *white*

Canepa Sauvignon Blanc 1993 Sagrada Familia   14   £C
A very well-turned-out sauvignon, with enough fruit to please the
palate and sufficient commanding acidity to tickle the taste-buds.

ENGLISH WINE – *white*

English House (Three Choirs Vineyards) n.v.   13   £C
A well-made wine, with fruit and acidity in good balance and
not sweet.

FRENCH WINE – *red*

Beaujolais Villages 1992 E. Loron   12   £C

**Bourgogne Passetoutgrain 1992 Vieilles Caves de
Bourgogne   12   £C**

Buzet 'Renaissance' 1991, Les Vignerons Buzet   13   £C
Tasty.

Cahors 1989   12   £C

Château Ducla 1991 Bordeaux   11   £C

Château Mingot Côtes de Castillon 1990   15   £C
Delicious. Contrives to be seriously dry and rich, yet amusingly
fruity and simply appealing. A very well-constructed wine.
Superb with roast foods.

Côtes de Gascogne n.v. 12 £B

Côtes du Frontonnais 1990 13 £C

Côtes du Roussillon 1993 13 £C

Domaine des Caunettes Hautes Cabardes 1989 16 £C
A terrific bargain here. A perfectly mature, bordeaux-type dry wine with rich, penetrating, smoothly achieved fruit of class and considerable style. Excellent roast-food, dinner-party wine.

Domaine St-Denis, Vin de Pays d'Oc, Cabernet Sauvignon n.v. 13 £C
Lots of attractive fruit here.

Fitou 1991 13 £C
Very appealing level of fruit.

Fitou Château de Segure 1989 14 £D
Perfect age. The fruit is still nicely earthy and heavy, but it's also smooth and beautifully rounded – yet very dry.

Mâcon Supérieur 1992, E. Loron 12 £C

Madiran 1988 Château de Crouseilles 13 £E
Expensive maturity. Dry fruit tending to sag at the edges just a smidgin, but good with rich food.

Mauregard Château la Jalgue 1992 13 £C
Some pleasant features to the fruit.

Michel Lynch Bordeaux Rouge 1990 12 £E
An overrated wine of some charm in the middle, but little effective structure either side. Very expensive for the paucity of style on offer.

Minervois Domaine de l'Estagnol n.v. 12 £B

Pinot Noir Cuvée a l'Ancienne 1989   10   £D

St-Joseph 1990 Louis Mousset   10   £E

Vieux Château Negrit, Montagne St-Émilion
1990   14   £D
Excellently put together. Will improve for two to three years
yet.

FRENCH WINE – *white*

Blanc de Blancs Yvon Mau n.v.   12   £B
Sound rather than exciting.

Buzet 'Renaissance' 1992, Les Vignerons de
Buzet   14   £C
Hugely attractive, decently priced wine, which comes across
with a delicious earthy undertone, like an expensive Côte du
Rhône blanc.

Chablis, Domaine de Corbeton 1992   10   £E
Faint asparagus hints in the fruit. Not classic, or very finely
tuned.

Chardonnay 1992, A. Bichot   11   £C

Château Ducla Entre-Deux-Mers 1992   12   £C

Côtes de Gascogne Domaine Lasserre du Haut
1992   12   £C

Mauregard Château les Marias Bordeaux Blanc
1992   13   £C
Reasonable fruit, some saline touches to the acidity. Good
with seafood.

**Muscadet de Sèvre-et-Maine Sur Lie Domaine de
Plessis n.v.** 12 £C

Pinot Blanc 1992 Woelfelin 14 £C
Delicious, fully formed pinot with rich fruit overtones and
some freshness. An excellent wine to enjoy by itself.

Sancerre Les Roches 1992, Vacheron 14 £E
An excellent sancerre, perfectly ripe and mature, with hints of
gooseberry, grass and melon with a clean finish. Classic, but
expensive.

Sauvignon Blanc 1993, Bordeaux 12 £C

**Vin de Pays d'Oc Chardonnay Domaine Colin Rosier
n.v.** 10 £C

GERMAN WINE – *white*

Hock n.v. 12 £A
Good value. And so much more acidically intriguing than
many liebfraumilchs.

**Mainzer Domherr Kabinett 1992, Mont Royal
Barois** 11 £C

HUNGARIAN WINE – *white*

Chardonnay 1993 Gyongyos Estate 14 £B
Delicious and lemony.

Sauvignon Blanc 1993 Gyongyos Estate   14   £B
Some attractive herbaceous fruit, nicely undercut by the
acidity. More characteristic of the grape than the '92.

ITALIAN WINE – *red*

Barbera del Piemonte 1992 Giordiano   13   £C
Good, sweet fruit.

Breganze 1992 Bartolomeo   13   £C

Merlot del Veneto 1992   12   £B

Montepulciano d'Abruzzo 1993 Miglianico   13   £C

ITALIAN WINE – *white*

Breganze 1993 Bartolomeo   12   £C

Orvieto Classico 1993 San Marco   12   £C

Pinot Grigio del Veneto 1992, Cesari   12   £C

Verdicchio dei Castelli di Jesi Classico 1993 11   £C

Via Nova, Tocai 1993   12   £C
Slight touch of the true apricot Tokay fruit.

PORTUGUESE WINE – *red*

Beira Mar Garrafeira 1980   15   £D
This belies its age with fruit so unwrinkled it's incredible. The Joan Collins of Portuguese wine.

Bora VQPRD 1992   14   £B

Dom Ferraz Reserva, Barraida 1989   13   £B

PORTUGUESE WINE – *white*

Bairrada Reserva 1992 'Dom Ferraz'   12   £C
Pleasant, lemony thing.

Dom Ferraz Reserva, Barraida 1993   13   £B

Vinho Verde 'Octave' Borges n.v.   10   £C

SOUTH AFRICAN WINE – *red*

Cape Cellars Cabernet Sauvignon 1992 Breede River Valley   13   £B
Very pleasant drinking. Friendly and soft – a teddy bear of a wine.

SOUTH AFRICAN WINE – *white*

Cape Cellars Chardonnay 1992 Coastal Region   12   £B

**Pearl Springs Sauvignon Blanc 1993, Breede
River Valley**   13   £B
Excellent value.

SPANISH WINE – *red*

Faustino Rivero Ulecia Rioja 1990   14   £C
Lots of chewy, rubbery, vanilla-tinged fruit which would be
marvellous with a vegetable or lamb curry.

La Mancha n.v.   15   £A
Brilliant value, quite brilliant. Soft (yet has enough tannic
presence to have backbone) and with oodles of fruit. Great
fun drinking.

SPANISH WINE – *white*

Castillo Fuentemayor Rioja 1989 Oak Aged   11   £C
Lots of wood and vanilla hiding the fruit, but disappearing
with creamy seafood dishes or grilled chicken.

El Coto Rioja 1992 Bodegas El Coto   13   £C
Curiously fresh rioja, good with shellfish.

La Mancha n.v.   13   £A
Terrific value party plonk.

USA WINE – *red*

Blossom Hill California   14   £C
Some sweet-finishing fruit here. Most lush and attractive.

**Columbia Crest Merlot 1990, Columbia Valley
Washington**   14   £E
Very pleasing, complex fruit: polished, soft and subtly rich.

USA WINE – *white*

Blossom Hill California n.v.   12   £C

SPARKLING WINE/CHAMPAGNE

**Clairette de Die Methode Dioise Ancestrale, Georges
Aubert n.v.**   13   £D
Good and peachy for sweet-toothed tipplers.

Duchatel Brut n.v.   13   £F
Not a bad bubbly.

'Mayerling' Crémant d'Alsace n.v.   14   £E
Like a fine-quality cava. Excellent value.

**Seaview Pinot Noir/Chardonnay 1990
(Australian)**   15   £E
Mature, fruity, classy. Great value.

Victoria Wine

I have received letters from *Guardian* readers telling me that Victoria Wine shops are not all alike. Mr and Mrs Hooson of Huntingdon unfortunately discovered that the branch of Victoria Wine they visited in St Ives disclaimed all knowledge of the marvellous bottles I had recommended and which the company's head office assured me were in stock. Mr Hooson felt sufficiently aggrieved to write to the *Guardian*'s editor suggesting that the paper 'refrain from recommending this chain of shops in the future' and I have every sympathy with his outrage. Interestingly, when the matter was dealt with by VW's HQ (efficiently and promptly, I might add), it was revealed that the clot in the shop 'was a part-time member not fully aware' and I pass on this insight to any other drinker who may one day be faced by a clueless wine-shop assistant. *It pays to demand to see the manager.*

Mr Thorp of London W11 certainly did when he wanted the same wines as Mr and Mrs Hooson and he was rewarded by two angels: Mr and Mrs Brooks. This seraphic pair manage the branch of Victoria Wine in Stratford Road, London W8, and provide 'helpfulness out of the ordinary'. They chased around finding the wines the customer wanted and weren't satisfied until Mr Thorp was.

It is maddening enough when a mute battery of supermarket shelving is deprived of a wine readers are dying to try, but when a shop assistant displays similar emptiness, muttering that he's never heard of the blessed bottle, then it is doubly galling. I hope that this occurrence will become the exception where readers are concerned because managers like the Brookses will not be.

If wine shops are to compete with supermarkets, then providing service by clued-up individuals has to be the area where they can notch up the highest brownie points. This is even more of an issue now because the supermarkets themselves are looking actively at putting wine advisers into their wine sections who can offer advice and help, on-the-spot tastings and a glass-hire service. Tesco is testing this idea out in three superstores at the moment, Marks and Spencer now have fifty wine shops within their larger stores, and if these enterprises are successful and expand, then it will only be so at the expense of wine shops. Supermarkets are not the places one thinks of when it comes to having civilized conversations and Victoria Wine are well placed to maintain the simple principles of this dying art.

They have 1,355 well-spread branches throughout England and Wales (and 178 in Scotland, called Haddows) and so there can be few urban-based folk who do not have a Victoria Wine establishment within striking distance, if not walking distance. Part of the problem with this particular chain from the customer's point of view is that not all its shops are wine shops: 642 are mere off-licences, 288 are what the chain calls a 'local shop' and these emporia do not carry the range a wine shop, of which there are 326, does. There are 87 establishments called Day Traders and, newest of all, 10 Victoria Wine Cellars shops. This diversity was, perhaps, at the heart of the problem encountered by my correspondents, although any shop with Victoria Wine on its front should be able to order any wine on the chain's list fairly quickly. For many people, however, Victoria Wine is just an 'offy' – an off-licence peddling beer and spirits as well as wine, not to mention fags (the chain sells millions of packets weekly), crisps and bars of chocolate. These products sit ill with the image of the wine merchant as a die-hard specialist replete with gaudy bow-tie, gouty left foot, and veined, furuncular nose. But then, thank goodness, Victoria Wine, in spite of the penny-black imagery, is not an olde worlde wine merchant. It is a very contemporary outfit.

Last year it did that very contemporary thing – it took over a competitor. This was the famous, or infamous if you will, Augustus Barnett. The 545 branches of this chain have now been integrated into the family. AB's strength is in its name and its image of cheapness, and if you ask me I'd introduce old Augustus to rapid euthanasia, turn all the shops which aren't geographically unsuitable into VW Cellar shops, and auction what's left. Make it quick, keep it simple, and give the competition something to think about. VW has already done this with the hiring of key executives with experience of what it's like to work for Tesco and Sainsbury. The new Wine Cellar shops – 10 opened in southern England in the early summer, 40 promised by the end of 1994 and a further 100 expected in 1995 – are an ideal place for the new blood to innovate and expand the empire. The range of services offered by the Cellar shops is wide and no competitor, I reckon, offers much more.

The chain has solid buying strengths to capitalize on any expansion plans. It is a lively shopper in the New World and the newly vibrant areas of the Old. It has its fair share of drinkable cheapies, is strong in the mid-price range, and is, I think, increasingly responsive to new ideas and will increasingly initiate projects with flying wine-makers and suchlike. In the final analysis, cheap wines will bring the customers in, but it's the reception they get which will keep them coming back.

Just as there are book lovers who feel intimidated by book-shops and so will buy all their reading matter at the larger branches of newsagents, there are wine lovers who feel uncomfortable in traditional wine merchants and prefer to make their purchases among unreproachful, unpoliced shelves. It is these drinkers the supermarkets have wooed so brilliantly, and the big challenge for the likes of Victoria Wine is not so much to increase their market share as to hold on to what they do have as the competition gets increasingly fierce. The way forward is clear: service from knowledgeable enthusiasts underpinning terrific wines costing well under a fiver with regular bargains under £3. Simple, isn't it?

ARGENTINIAN WINE – *red*

Las Alturas Red, J. Lurton 1993   11 £C

ARGENTINIAN WINE – *white*

Las Alturas White, J. Lurton 1993   13 £C

AUSTRALIAN WINE – *red*

Basedow Cabernet Sauvignon 1992   17 £D
Creamy, digestive-biscuit middle to this impressive wine, which is aromatic fore and ripely sweet aft. Superb. Available from Victoria Wine Cellars and Wine Shops.

Basedow Shiraz 1993   16 £D
Blackberry, raspberry, dry, plummy – it's got the lot, with a

shroud of rich figs. Available from Victoria Wine Cellars and Wine Shops.

Brown Brothers Shiraz/Cabernet 1983   14   £E
Good price for such a mature, teeth-grippingly (yet soft) tannic performance. Floods of flavour and style. Available from Victoria Wine Cellars and Wine Shops.

Brown Brothers Tarrango 1993   15   £C
Vivid, striking, softly smoky and rubbery, and so gluggable it's indecent.

Deakin Estate Cabernet Sauvignon 1993   14   £C
Complex, multi-layered, rich fruit, with almost a Marmite touch on the finish. Delicious and characterful.

Hardy's Cabernet/Shiraz Stamp Series 1992   14   £B
Some steamed fruit and soft spice – good big, pasta, party wine.

Katnook Cabernet Sauvignon 1990   14   £E
Expressive but expensive. Available from Victoria Wine Cellars and Wine Shops.

Katnook Merlot 1990   15   £E
Ripely integrated fruit character which is softly tannic and flavourful. Available from Victoria Wine Cellars and Wine shops.

Nottage Hill Cabernet Sauvignon 1992   15   £C
Still sporting a day-old growth of beard to the smooth fruit (courtesy of the tannins). Lovely performer – one of the best-made cabernet sauvignons around for the money.

Penfolds Bin 35 Shiraz Cabernet 1992   15   £C
Ripe, soft fruit with some development ahead of it. Attractive berry flavours, well-structured and balanced. Very drinkable now, but a 17–18-pointer in three to four years.

**Penfolds Coonawarra Cabernet Sauvignon
1990**   17   £E
The colour of crushed blackberries, subtle eucalyptus/leather
aroma, sheer-satiny acids and velvet-textured fruit touches –
lovely tannicky finish.

Riddoch Shiraz 1992   15   £D
Soft, spicy fruit, initially dry then turning soft, this is a handsome specimen.

Ryecroft Peppertree Shiraz/Cabernet 1990   16   £D
Lovely touches to the dry structure of the fruit, which then
finishes sweetly lush. Delicious.

**Woodford Hill Cabernet Sauvignon/Shiraz
1992**   13   £C
Good and fruity, with some well-intentioned fruit.

**Woodford Hill Shiraz/Cabernet Sauvignon
1991**   15   £C
Specially selected for Augustus Barnett. Great value. Smoky-
edged, rich fruit, soft, not spicy, gingery or hard, but comfortable and accommodating. Delicious.

AUSTRALIAN WINE – *white*

Basedow Chardonnay 1993   15   £D
Big, brassy, rich – like a Texan oil millionaire. Available in
Victoria Wine Cellars and Wine Shops.

Basedow Semillon 1993   15   £D
Woody and rich. Probably magnificent with lemon chicken.
Available in Victoria Wine Cellars and Wine Shops.

Cape View Sauvignon Blanc, K. Milne 1993   13   £C

Chapel Hill Rhein Riesling, K. Milne 1992   12   £B
Light aperitif.

Deakin Estate Chardonnay 1993   14   £C
A well-balanced, quiet Chardonnay, delicious as an aperitif.

Deakin Estate Colombard/Chardonnay 1993   13   £C
Pleasant, very effective combination of grapes.

Deakin Estate Sauvignon Blanc 1993   13   £C

Hardy's Moondah Brook Verdelho 1993   14 to 16   £D
Highly attractive aperitif. Rates 16 with a fish salad with bitter
leaves and a lemony dressing.

**Katnook Botrytised Chardonnay 1992 (half-
bottle)**   13   £D
Rich and very honeyed, but not complex enough yet – maybe
in two years? Available from Victoria Wine Cellars and Wine
Shops.

Nottage Hill Chardonnay 1993   15   £C
Lovely stuff. Has firmness of fruit, delicacy of acidity and
decisiveness of structure – without being blowsy or offensively
overripe.

Oxford Landing Sauvignon Blanc 1993   14   £C

Penfolds Bin 21 Semillon/Chardonnay 1993   15   £C
Fresh and lively, yet a dollop of pineappley melon keeps
intruding. Delicious, refreshing wine.

Penfolds Koonunga Hill Chardonnay 1992   14   £C
Full, lush fruit plus a ticklish dollop of lemon zest. Delicious,
but getting pricey near a fiver.

Rowan Chardonnay, Victoria 1992 14 £D
Some sweet fruit on the finish. Good wood integration and
style to the overall structure.

BULGARIAN WINE – *red*

Bear Ridge Gamza n.v. 12 £B

Debut Cabernet Sauvignon 1993 13 £B
Very sound.

BULGARIAN WINE – *white*

Bear Ridge Bulgarian Dry White 1993 13 £B

Bear Ridge Chardonnay n.v. 13 £B
Pleasant, inoffensive, fruity.

CHILEAN WINE – *red*

Caliterra Cabernet Sauvignon 1991 16 £C
Dry, lovely dry-blackcurrant fruit. Very classically moulded
and finished.

Montes Alpha Cabernet Sauvignon 1989 14 £E
Big and will be bigger. Put down for two to three years.

CHILEAN WINE – *white*

Caliterra Sauvignon Blanc 1994   16 £C
Delicate and grassy lemon aromas, with a refined finish of soft
melon on the fruit. Lovely wine at a lovely price.

Villa Montes Sauvignon Blanc, H. Ryman 1993   13 £C

ENGLISH WINE – *white*

Penn Vineyards Dry 1993, English White   12 £D
Expensive. A feeble finish to an otherwise good wine mars the
performance.

FRENCH WINE – *red*

**Alsace Pinot Noir Cuvée Medaillon d'Or
Pfaffenheim 1992**   14 £D
Rich, gamy fruit with raspberry undertones. Delicious chilled.
Available from Victoria Wine Cellars.

Beaujolais, Philippe de Coucelettes 1993   14 £C
I am compelled to admit I liked this modern bubble-gum-
fruity beaujolais more than I thought possible.

Beaujolais Villages, Jouet 1993   12 £C

Big Frank's Red n.v.   15 £D
Is big and frank; has complex, tannic fruit; hugely drinkable
and rich. Rather jaunty name with a wine to match. Available

from Victoria Wine Cellars and Wine Shops.

Château Carignan, Bordeaux 1990 13 £D
This will soften and improve in bottle for a little while yet.

**Château de Mercey, Mercurey Premier Cru
1990** 13 £F
Available from Victoria Wine Cellars.

**Château La Diffre, Seguret, Côtes du Rhône
Villages 1992** 12 £C
Put down for a year.

Château La Grave, Bordeaux 1991 11 £C

**Château Ormières, Minervois, J. P. Ormières
1991** 14 £C
Some soft, very approachable fruit, fresh and vigorous in feel,
yet mature and a mite serious at heart. Good value.

Château Vaudieu, Châteauneuf-du-Pape 1990 14 £E
Good.

**Château Vrai Caillou, Bordeaux Supérieur
1989** 13 £C
Attractive tannins here.

Clos Fortet 1988 15 £G
Distinguished, bold, hunky, rich. Very big and aristocratic.
Available from Victoria Wine Cellars.

Cornas, Allemand 1991 16 £G
Big, thumping, hairy-chested brute with soft berries, brambly
and rich, mingling with chocolate and figs. Only the price is
cause for regret. Available from Victoria Wine Cellars.

Côtes de Brouilly, Philippe de Coucelettes 1993 11 £D
Available from Victoria Wine Cellars and Wine Shops.

Domaine de Bigarnon 1983   14   £F
Delicious, classic, very dry, yet mature. Probably not an out-
rageous price for an eleven-year-old. Available from Victoria
Wine Cellars.

**Domaine de Rivoyre, Vin de Pays d'Oc, Cabernet
Sauvignon H. Ryman 1990**   13   £C

**Domaine de St-Laurent, Vin de Pays des
Coteaux du Libron 1993**   14   £B

**Domaine de St-Laurent, Vin de Pays des
Coteaux du Libron 1992**   11   £B

Domaine Sallele Syrah 1993   14   £B
Good, rounded fruit.

Domaine Sallele, Vin de Pays d'Oc Syrah, 1992 12   £B

Fitou Mme C. Parmentier n.v.   12   £C

Fleurie, Georges Duboeuf 1992   11   £D

French Full Red Vin de Pays de l'Herault   13   £B
Delicious. Excellent value. Simple but effective. Also available
in 1.5 litres for £5.89.

Hautes Côtes de Beaune, Dennis Carre 1992   13   £D
Available from Victoria Wine Cellars.

**Hautes Côtes de Nuits, Oak Aged, Les Caves
des Hautes Côtes 1992**   14   £D
Interesting wine. Not classic pinot noir, but an impressive red
for all that. Available from Victoria Wine Cellars and Wine
Shops.

La Serre, Syrah Vin de Pays d'Oc 1992   10   £C

Michel Lynch Bordeaux Rouge 1990 12 £E

An overrated wine of some charm in the middle, but little effective structure either side. Very expensive for the paucity of style on offer.

Minervois Caves des Hautes Coteaux 13 £B

Morgon, Les Vignerons du Prieure 1993 11 £D

Available from Victoria Wine Cellars and Wine Shops.

Nuits St-Georges, Clos St Marc 1988 13 £G

Available from Victoria Wine Cellars.

Sancerre Rouge, Domaine de Montigny, Henri Natter 1989 16 £E

Proof that Monsieur Natter can make not only the most refined sancerre blanc, but an equally impressive rouge. Dry, rich, weighty, with lots of complex fruit. Available from Victoria Wine Cellars.

St-Romain, Bernard Fevre 1990 11 £D

Vin de Pays de Vaucluse Red, La Mission 1993 14.5 £B

Bargain polished-fruit number. Lots of swirling flavours, rather muted aromatically, but very sound for the money.

FRENCH WINE – *white*

Angelico 1993, Calvet 14 £C

Soft, ripe fruit chiming nicely and freshly and in a very contemporary style. First Calvet wine I've liked overmuch.

Bourgogne Chardonnay, Boisset Charles de France, Boisset 1992   13   £C
Some class, but not a lot of grip and woodily indistinct.

Chablis Premier Cru, Les Vaudevey, Bacheroy-Josselin 1992   15   £E
Classy stuff, with enough weight of fruit yet cut of acid, beautifully in step, to please any chablis freak.

Chardonnay de Bourgogne, Charles de France Boisset n.v.   12   £C

Château de Vaudieu Blanc, Châteauneuf-du-Pape 1993   14   £E
Delicious touch of soft earthiness to the vigorous fruit, which is impressive without being overstated.

Château Filhot Deuxième Cru Sauternes 1988   16   £G
Magnificent balanced, rich wine. A real treat. Has rich, sweet fruit that has layers of complexity and flavour. Available from Victoria Wine Cellars.

Château La Diffre, Seguret Côtes du Rhône Villages 1993   12   £C

Domaine de la Croix Bergerac, H. Ryman 1992   12   £C
Rather muted and dumb for the eloquent Mr Ryman.

Domaine de la Tuilerie Chardonnay Vin de Pays d'Oc 1992   14   £C
Delicious touches to the fruit.

Domaine de la Tuilerie Vin de Pays d'Oc, H. Ryman 1992   13   £C
OK, but not very entertaining or inviting.

Domaine l'Argentier Terret, Vin de Pays Côtes de Thau 1993   14 £B
Available in Victoria Wine Cellars and Wine Shops.

Domaine le Ploges, Vin de Pays d'Oc, Chasan 1992   13 £C
Very pleasant, inoffensive, light, with some touches of good fruit.

Gaillac Blanc, Cave de Labastide de Levis 1992   12 £B

Gewürztraminer, Cave Vinicole de Turckheim 1992   13 £C
Lay down for three years. Rich, but not balanced yet.

La Serre Sauvignon 1992   12 £C

Muscat de Rivesaltes Mimosas, Dessert Wine n.v. (half-bottle)   10 £B
This wine, usually an outstanding honey monster, is, in this example, curiously waxy and almost soapy in feel.

Muscat Sec Domaine de Montrabech n.v.   11 £C

Pouilly-Fuissé, Duvergey-Taboureau 1993   12 £E
Available in Victoria Wine Cellars and Wine Shops.

Sancerre Cuvée de Chene de St-Louis 1992   12 £D

Sur Lie, Vin de Pays d'Oc, Mme C. Parmentier 1992   13 £C
Good pear-drop fresh fruit. What a pity it's not £2.99!

Syrah Rosé Fortant de France 1993   13 £C

Vin de Pays de l'Herault French Dry White   13 £B
There's a touch of sweet-and-sour fruit on the rather loose edge. Good value, but somewhat limp in the final analysis, though fish and chips will work well with it.

Vin de Pays de Vaucluse Blanc, La Mission
1993   15 £B
Elegant labelling, discreet, refined, yet purposeful and this
stands for the wine as well.

GERMAN WINE – *white*

Bad Kreuznacher Kahlenberg Riesling Spätlese,
1988   10 £D
You said it. Dull, sweet, uninteresting.

Deidesheimer Hergottsacker Riesling Spätlese
Winzerverein Niederkirchen 1988   15 £C
Full of brilliant, delicious fruit. Great with creamy fish dishes.

Dexheimer Doktor Scheurebe Kabinett,
Rheinfront 1988   16 £B
Gorgeous muted-elderberry nose and fruit; some floral
sweetness on the finish. Fantastic value for watching TV with.

Falkensteiner Hofberg Riesling Kabinett
Friedrich Wilhelm Gymnasium 1988   15 £C
Real paint-stripper nose, but four-star-Shell citrus fruit – a
good, classic riesling. Brilliant aperitif at a good age.

Forster Jesuitengarten Riesling Spätlese 1988   10 £E
Uninteresting, why bother?

Friedelsheimer Kruez Gewürztraminer Spätlese,
Vollmer 1991   13 £D

Gaubischofheimer Herrenberg Spätlese
Schulz-Werner 1988   10 £D
Dull, sweet, usual thing.

Kabinette, Bornheimer Adelberg 1992 10 £B

Munsterer Pittersberg Riesling Kabinett, Staatl, Weinbau Schloss Bockelheim 1988 14 £D
Wholemeal-loaf nose, rowany fruit, soft.

Niederhauser Hermanshole Riesling Spätlese Staatl, Weinbau Schloss Bockelheim 1988 15 £D
Lush fruit, vividly soft and tongue lashing. A rich tipple at bedtime.

Serriger Heiligenborn Riesling Spätlese 1983 10 £D

Serriger Herrenberg Riesling Spätlese, Bert Simon 1985 10 £D
Excites me not a jot.

Spätlese, Bornheimer Adelberg 1990 13 £B
Not a bad aperitif.

Trittenheimer Apotheke Riesling Auslese, Friedrich Wilhelm Gymnasium 1988 14 £E
Lovely aroma of muted lemon sherbet – rich fruit with a petally echo. A wine for cheese and a bunch of grapes.

HUNGARIAN WINE – *red*

Cabernet Sauvignon Szekszard n.v. 14 £B
Soft and flavoursome.

Country Red Villany 1993 13 £B
Attractive, bustling fruit.

Merlot, Szekszard Minosegi n.v. 14 £B
Rich, suede-edged, flavourful fruit. Great value.

HUNGARIAN WINE – *white*

Chapel Hill Irsay Oliver n.v.	11	£B
Chapel Hill Rhein Riesling 1993	12	£B
Chapel Hill Sauvignon Blanc 1993	12	£B
Chardonnay Balaton 1993	11	£B
Country White Magyar Vineyards n.v.	11	£B
Gyongyos Sauvignon Blanc H. Ryman n.v. Real gooseberry character.	13	£B
Oak Forest Chardonnay 1993	12	£B

ITALIAN WINE – *red*

Aglianico del Vulture, Riserva, Pipoli 1986   14 £D
Perfect cheese wine with its ripe maturity and well-finished fruit/acid balance.

Chianti Rufina Riserva, Fattoria di Gaglia 1990   15 £C
Lovely, dry, tannic (but very friendly) earthy, full of flavoursome fruit.

**Colle del Talo, Vino da Tavola, Castello
Vicchiomaggio** 1990   14 £D
Prunes and violets, rich, dark, satisfying, classy, well-balanced.

Cortenova Merlot 13 n.v.   13 £B
Some attractive fruit with faint savoury echoes.

Corvina, Vino da Tavola di Verona, Pasqua
1992 13 £B
Pleasant soft fruit, balanced, attractive. Not a lot more.

Lambrusco Secco, Tenuta Generale Cialdini
1992 14 £B
The real thing imported without the sparkling wine capsule, so it attracts a lower duty rate. This is a deliciously zippy red. Great with cold meats and salads. Chill it.

Merlot/Sangiovese, Casal del Giglio 1993 16 £B
Black cherries, plums and blackberries, with a shroud of rich tannin. Austere, but very impressive. Interesting and very successful marriage of French and Italian grapes: dry, firmly fruity, balanced, very effectively built from first to last. Available from Victoria Wine Cellars and Wine Shops.

Pellegrino Ruby Marsala n.v. 14 £D
Try it with baked apples and custard. Available from Victoria Wine Cellars and Wine Shops.

Primitivo del Salento, Le Trulle 1993 14 £C
Gamy, rich aromas and initial fruit attack, then nicely ripe cherries. Delicious.

Sangiovese di Toscana, Cecchi 1992 14 £B
Agreeable introduction to earthy chianti by nature, if not in name.

Squinzano, Mottura n.v. 13 £B
Pleasing fruity lift to the fruit on the finish.

Toar, Vino da Tavola, Masi 1990 14 £E
Fabulous, teeth-gripping fruit.

Valpolicella Classico Zonin 'Il Maso', 1991 14 £C
Seriously good, dry, black-cherry fruit here.

Valpolicella Pasqua 1992   11   £B
Cherry mouth-wash.

Vermiglio di Ripanera, Vino da Tavola n.v.   14   £C
Delicious. Soft, plummy fruit of vivid freshness.

**Vigneti di Marano, Amarone della Valpolicella,
Boscaini 1990**   14   £E
Acquired taste, but worth acquiring: almondy, cherryish, dry,
yet very soft with a hint of raisin. Available from Victoria Wine
Cellars.

ITALIAN WINE – *white*

Bianco di Custoza 1993   12   £B
Lemony, light.

**Chardonnay de Salento, Vigneto di Caramia
1993**   14   £D
Expensive, but the fruit is rich, the structure sound, the effect
satisfying. Available in Victoria Wine Cellars only.

Chardonnay del Piemonte Castelvero 1992   11   £C

Chardonnay del Salento, 'Le Trulle' n.v.   14   £C
Very pleasing balance of fruit and acid. Almost a class act.

Dry Muscate di Puglia 'Le Trulle' 1993   13   £B
Delicious little aperitif.

Lugana, Pasqua 1993   13   £C
Elegant lemony wine.

Pellegrino Superiore Secco Marsala n.v.   14   £D
An elegant, hugely original and sophisticated aperitif. Available from Victoria Wine Cellars.

Puglian Rosé 'Le Trulle' 1993   12   £B

Soave Classico Superiore, Anselmi 1993   13   £D
This is a delicious and gracefully forward soave, but such is the pricey pretension of its two labels that you wonder if the fortune this added to the price couldn't have been better used reducing it. Available in Victoria Wine Cellars only.

Soave, Pasqua n.v.   13   £B
Not bad, not great – but not bad for dear old soave, which in this example at least is neither dear nor old.

Verdicchio Classico Villa Pigna 1993   12   £C
Available in Victoria Wine Cellars and Wine Shops.

Villa Fontana, Fontana Candida 1992   13   £C
One of the better examples of frascati.

MORAVIAN WINE – *red*

Moravia Hills Dry Red n .v.   13   £B

MORAVIAN WINE – *white*

Moravia Hills Dry White n.v.   12   £B

NEW ZEALAND WINE – *red*

Corbans Merlot 1992   15   £E
Curious clotted-cream-and-raspberry-meringue fruit. Rather
delicious. Available from Victoria Wine Cellars and Wine
Shops.

Stoneleigh Cabernet Sauvignon 1993   13   £D

Vidal Hawkes Bay Cabernet/Merlot 1992   13   £E
This has sweetly impressive fruit, but sourly unimpressive
price tag. Available from Victoria Wine Cellars and Wine
Shops.

NEW ZEALAND WINE – *white*

Colonnade Chardonnay 1993   14   £D
Available in Victoria Wine Cellars and Wine Shops.

Nobilo Sauvignon Blanc 1993   14   £D
Delicious ripe (lychee and pear) touch to the typical herbaceous fruit.

Stoneleigh Sauvignon Blanc 1993   13   £D
Very grassy, very clean, very fresh. Good with oysters.

Vidal Hawkes Bay Sauvignon Blanc 1993   14   £D
Slightly honeyed undertones on the grassiness we have come
to expect of New Zealand sauvignon blancs. Distinguished
feel to the fruit. Delicious with grilled fish. Available in Victoria Wine Cellars and Wine Shops.

PORTUGUESE WINE – *red*

Borba VQPRD 1992   14   £B

Cave do Duque n.v. (1 litre)   10   £B

Garrafeira TE, Fonseca 1988   15   £D
Blackberry crumble and strawberry jam. Available from Victoria Wine Cellars and off-licences.

Grão Vasco, Dão, Sogrape 1990   13   £C
Available from Victoria Wine Cellars and Wine Shops.

Leziria, Adega Co-operative de Almeirim n.v.   14   £B
Touch drier than before, but still excellent cherryish fruit and good value.

Quinta de Camarate, Fonseca 1989   15   £C
Lots of ripe figs and black cherries. Delicious. Available from Victoria Wine Cellars and Wine Shops.

Warres Quinta de Cavadinha 1982   16   £G
Prunes (armagnac-flavoured), figs and cream. Rich, very rich, impossibly rich, smoky finish. Lovely port.

PORTUGUESE WINE – *white*

Bairrada Reserva, Sogrape 1991   15   £C
Extremely rich, rounded fruit which is not refined, but certainly impressive. Available in Victoria Wine Cellars and Wine Shops.

Chello, Dry Vinho Verde 1993   13 £C
Spritzy and fresh, earthy echoes. Very good appetite tickler.

Leziria Dry, Co-operative de Almeirim 1993   14 £B
Favourite tasty, good value, Portuguese wine.

Leziria Medium Dry White, Almeirim n.v.   12 £B

Moscatel de Setubal Fonseca 1989   16.5 £D
Bargain, deeply fruited pud wine with overtones of sweet, ripe
melon and muscaty figs. Available from Victoria Wine Cellars.

Quinta de Azevedo Vinho Verde 1993   14 £C
Has a delicious prickle and acidic lift to the fruit, which is
present if not clamorous. Available in Victoria Wine Cellars
and Wine Shops.

SOUTH AFRICAN WINE – *red*

Belvedere du Cap Syrah 1994   14 £C
Modern, fruit-drop fruit surrounding a dry core. Good pizza
wine. Available from Victoria Wine Cellars and Wine Shops.

Cape View Cinsault/Shiraz 1993   14 £B
Rich and well-balanced. Not always concomitant attributes.

Cape View Cinsault/Shiraz, K. Milne 1993   12 £B

Cape View Merlot, K. Milne 1993   14 £C
Very soft, minty merlot. Delicious, cushy style of fruit. Good
pasta wine. Further evidence that merlot in the Cape has a
great future.

Neethlingshof Pinotage 1984   14 £D
Mature, yet far from middle-aged. Has suppleness of fruit,

vigour of flavour and staying power. Available from Victoria
Wine Cellars.

Saxenburg Cabernet Sauvignon 1991 13 £D
Available from Victoria Wine Cellars and Wine Shops.

Stellenzicht Cabernet/Malbec 1992 14 £C
Smooth yet craggy. Available from Victoria Wine Cellars and
Wine Shops.

Stellenzicht Cabernet/Malbec 1992 14 £C
Smooth yet craggy. Available from Victoria Wine Cellars and
Wine Shops.

SOUTH AFRICAN WINE – *white*

Cape View Chardonnay Sur Lie 1994 13 £C

Cape View Sauvignon Blanc 1993 14 £C
Excellent. Has a rich gooseberry and melon touch to the fruit,
yet is fresh and crisp. Superb grilled-fish wine.

Cape White 1994 14 £B
Soft fruit here. Terrific little glug.

Cathedral Cellars Sauvignon Blanc 1993 13 £D
Available from Victoria Wine Cellars and Wine Shops.

Chenin Blanc Simonsvlei 1994 14 £B
Fabulous pear-drop, party wine.

Goiya Kgeisje 1994 14 £C
A sauvignon blanc/chardonnay combination with a lovely
fruity backbone and excellent structure. The addition of chardonnay has filled out the wine yet kept masses of freshness

and citric flavour, and it is terrific fun drinking. One of the
first '94-vintage wines on sale. It also sports the most attractively original, and apposite, wine label I've seen in years, with
perfectly weighted and designed typography and a superbly
vibrant representation of a dove. Available from Victoria Wine
Cellars and Wine Shops.

Neethlingshof Gewürztraminer 1994   13 £C
A pleasant, rosy-fruited aperitif. Available in Victoria Wine
Cellars and Wine Shops.

Shiraz Blanc de Noirs, Van Loveren 1994   14 £C
A subtle rosé wine, dry and deliciously drinkable. An excellent
aperitif. Available in Victoria Wine Cellars and Wine Shops.

Stellenzicht Sauvignon/Chardonnay 1992   14 £C
Impressive. The chardonnay of the two takes the lead, but it's
an effective partnership, enriching both parties.

SPANISH WINE – *red*

Campo Viejo Rioja Gran Reserva 1982   15 £D
Perfect weight of supple-limbed, ripe yet not heavy fruit.
Available from Victoria Wine Shops.

Campo Viejo Rioja Reserva 1987   14 £C
Delicious – formal, but delicious. Available from Victoria
Wine Shops and Off-Licences.

Casa Barco, Oaked Red, Vino de Mesa n.v.   14 £B
Rustic wine with its fruit, and its price, firmly on the ground.

Chivite Reserva Navarra 1989 14 £C
A classic tempranillo and garnacha blend of good richness,
which only fails to knock up more points because the finish is
not as purposeful as the initial attack.

CVNE Viña Real Rioja 1989 (half-bottle) 14 £B
Delicious half which delivers the whole dry, rich fruit. Available from Victoria Wine Shops.

Gandia Cabernet Sauvignon 13 £B
Has little varietal fidelity which normally I wouldn't give a
monkey's about, but if a wine is advertised as being of such
and such a grape variety, we are entitled, I think, to expect to
find some echo of this grape's character in the wine. The wine
is not as forceful as it might be, but it is hale in all other
respects and makes itself perfectly at home with pasta.

Gandia Merlot n.v. 14 £B
The merlot is softer and more characteristic than the cab/
sauv, with a suggestion of rich vegetality to the fruit, and is
most definitely a cheerful companion to food.

Gandia Tempranillo n.v. 14 £B
Nicely woody and gently blackcurranty, and these factors
combine to make it very approachable; an attractive goggle-
box glug.

Las Torres Merlot 1992 13 £D
Expensive for the relative simplicity of the style. Available
from Victoria Wine Cellars and Wine Shops.

Palacio de Leon 1989 14 £B
Soft fruit, chocolate touches, with nicely developing tannins.
Good roast-food wine.

Puerta de la Villa 1993   15   £B

An outstanding tempranillo wine from Valdepeñas. Superb
cherry/raspberry/plum fruit with a lovely, serious, dry
finishing touch. Great value for deliciously polished fruit.

Raimat Tempranillo 1990   15   £D

The '89 vintage of this was pleasing, but this newly released
vintage is deeper and more complex and an altogether more
charismatic bottle. It exhibits velvety berried fruits with a
lovely balancing acidity and has delightfully soft fruit tannins
and integrated wood tannins. It will age with great grace, this
wine, and I see no reason, though it is delicious now, not to
expect it to improve and lengthen its fruit over the next
half-decade and more – should anyone possess the saintly
strength of will to keep from quaffing it. It rates 15 points now
and with a few years' bottle age may well be knocking on 17's
door.

Red Charcelo 1990   15   £C

This delightful Spanish red wine is a shining example of a
once best-avoided breed called Jumilla – an area which for
many years sulkily rejoiced in the reputation of being to wine
areas what Benidorm is to holiday resorts (no mere coincidence, since Benidorm is just down the road). It is a soft, dry
wine with a delicious hint of dried raspberry on the finish, this
last flourish doubtless a contribution from its twelve months
spent lounging in oak barrels. Since the blend is 40 per cent
monastrell, 30 per cent cabernet sauvignon and 30 per cent
tempranillo, it probably needed time to soften in wood, for
monastrell is no soft touch as a grape, being the progeny of a
vine so tough that it eats phylloxera (the most feared vine bug
on earth) for breakfast, rather than the other way round.
Charcelo is a delightful straightforward glug of uncluttered
fruit and I love it.

Rivarey Rioja 1992 14 £C
Excellent new-style rioja with, I would guess, garnacha
(French grenache) as the dominant variety. A superb earthy
fruitiness is the result.

SPANISH WINE – *white*

J. F. Lurton Rosado 1993, Tempranillo 14 £C
Cheerful, tasty rosé of some appeal. Available in Victoria
Wine Shops only.

Rivarey Oaked Rioja n.v. 12 £C
Good with spicy and/or creamy fish dishes.

Rueda Hermanos Lurton n.v. 14 £C
Delicious aperitif.

Torres Gran Viña Sol, Chardonnay 1992 14 £D
Well-constructed, naturally fruity and has a classy feel. Available in Victoria Wine Cellars and Wine Shops.

USA WINE – *red*

Stratford Pinot Noir n.v. 13 £C
Cherries – soft, gamy cherries.

Stratford Zinfandel n.v. 13 £C
Cinnamon and allspice-flavoured fruit.

USA WINE – *white*

Corbett Canyon Chardonnay 1992   14 £C
More controlled than previous vintages which have tended
towards being blowsy.

**Essensia Orange Muscat Halves 1992, Andrew Quady
(half-bottle)**   14 £D
Extraordinary stuff. Superbly rich and sweet and great with
strawberry tart.

SPARKLING WINE/CHAMPAGNE

Amelie Sebastien, Brut Champagne n.v.   14 £E
Good value.

Anna de Codorniu, Chardonnay 1989   15 £E
One of the most elegant fizzers on sale. A fine alternative to
good champagne. Very classic style of fruit and acid. Prices
differ between Victoria Wine and Augustus Barnett.

Clairette de Die Cuvée Cybele n.v.   13 £D
Great peachy fun for the honey-dentured.

**Crémant d'Alsace Cuvée Julien, Dopff n.v.
(French)**   15 £E
As expensive, but better than many a cheap champagne.
Available from Victoria Wine Cellars.

**Crémant de Bourgogne, Blanc de Noirs, Caves
de Bailly n.v. (French)**   15 £D
Brilliant softish fruit with firm acids: excellent value. Available
from Victoria Wine Cellars and Wine Shops.

Croser Sparkling 1991 (Australian)　　13　£F
Available from Victoria Wine Cellars.

Graham Beck, Brut n.v.　　13　£D

Heritage Sparkling Brut n.v.　　14　£E
Thoroughly well-made, decent, subtly citric bubbly. Shock the frogs with it.

Maison La Motte, Chardonnay n.v.　　13　£E

Marqués de Monistrol Brut Rosé n.v. (Spanish)　14　£E
Elegant. Available from Victoria Wine Cellars.

Marquis de la Tour Brut, Ackerman n.v.　　14　£B
Brilliant apple-skin-flavoured sparkler of dash and verve.

Marquis de la Tour Brut n.v. (French)　　14　£C
The largest-selling bubbly in the shop and no wonder if you like off-dry, peachy fruit. An excellent aperitif.

Paul d'Hurville, Brut Champagne n.v.　　15　£E
Lovely fruit sparkler. Great style and price.

Pelorus 1989 (New Zealand)　　13　£F
Available from Victoria Wine Cellars.

Raimat Sparkling Chardonnay, Brut n.v.　　13　£D

Seppelt Great Western Brut n.v. (Australia)　　16　£C
Superb bargain. A finer fizzer on sale for under a fiver it's difficult to name. Lemony, zingy, zesty. Great style.

Seppelt Salinger Sparkling Wine n.v. (Australia)　　15　£F
Mature, yet fresh finishing. Some elegance. Dry.

Seppelt Sparkling Shiraz 1990　　16　£E
Fabulous, roaring fruit.

Sparkling Chardonnay, Barbero n.v. (Italian)   13   £C
Pleasant and inoffensive. Available from Victoria Wine
Cellars and Wine Shops.

Torre del Gall Brut 1990   14   £E
Excellent. Has an underlying richness of fruit class.

Vintage Champagne 1986 (Victoria Wine)   14   £G
Rich and fulfilling. Balanced, stylish, classy.

Rating guide

10, 11   Nothing nasty but equally nothing worth shouting from the rooftops. Drinkable.

12, 13   Above average, interestingly made. A bargain taste.

14, 15, 16   This is the exceptional stuff, from the very good to the brilliant.

17, 18   Really great wine, worthy of individual acclaim. The sort of wine you can decant and serve to ignorant snobs who'll think it famous even when it is no such thing.

19, 20   Overwhelmingly marvellous. Wine which cannot be faulted, providing an experience never to be forgotten.

PRICE BANDS

A Under £2.50   E £7.00–£10.00

B £2.50–£3.50   F £10.00–£13.00

C £3.50–£5.00   G £13.00–£20.00

D £5.00–£7.00   H Over £20.00